MAN'S WISDOM
or
GOD'S WISDOM

**Concerning The Cause and Remedy
of Mental, Emotional, and
Behavioral Issues**

John T. Cocoris, Th.M., M.A., Psy.D.

Man's Wisdom or God's Wisdom
© Temperament Dynamics, LLC
By John T. Cocoris, Th.M., M.A., Psy.D.

© Temperament Dynamics, LLC
4848 Lemmon Ave.
STE 152
Dallas, TX 75219

www.discstrengths.com
info@discstrengths.com
512-553-8104

Library of Congress Card Number:
ISBN: 978-1-948474-09-2
9-10-25

Temperament Dynamics, LLC
Dallas, Texas 75219

**Cover design and interior design and layout by
John T. Cocoris**

Printed in the United States of America

Table of Contents

Preface

PART III Temperaments, Psychology, & Counseling

PART IV God's Wisdom

Preface

This book is written from a Biblical point of view. I am offering a common sense understanding of mental health issues such as anxiety, depression, bipolar, etc. Here is my background and experience that led me to writing this book.

I entered Christian ministry and pastored several churches in the 1970s and 1980s. I was a licensed therapist for twenty-five years. To obtain my license, I did a two year internship working with people who had Multiple Personalities (DID: Dissociative Identity Disorder). I worked in a mental hospital for three years. I worked with people who had issues like anxiety, panic attacks, depression, drug and alcohol addictions, bipolar disorder, schizophrenia, multiple personalities, etc.

I worked with all ages from children to senior citizens. While working at the mental hospital I made 957 visits to area hospitals in Dallas, Texas to evaluate people that presented to an emergency room with a mental issue. My job was to determine if the person needed to be committed for treatment.

As a therapist in private practice, I worked with individuals and couples that had relationship issues, those who were bipolar, those with anxiety, depression, and more.

I have been a corporate consultant since 1984. I have authored nine books, and a twelve workbook series.

Throughout my lifetime I have been driven to understand why we have problems of any kind and what treatment is best to restore normalcy.

My desire for the ministry and to help people led me to obtain a masters degree in theology, a master's degree in counseling, and a doctorate in psychology.

As a Christian, grounded in Scripture, I have a Biblical view of man. The Biblical view of man is in direct contrast to the world's view of a human being.

Prevailing thought from man's wisdom is that a person is the product of his environment, genetics, and/or brain chemistry. Once this is accepted, it is easy to conclude that a person is a victim of his or her circumstances and they are therefore not responsible or accountable for their behavior.

In contrast, the Bible is clear that man is made in God's image possessing mind, emotion, and will. Biblically, we are held responsible and accountable for what we think, feel, say, and do. We are the product of the choices we make.

Along my journey I discovered the oldest system known to man that describes why we do what we do and it greatly influenced my understanding of human behavior. It dates back over 2,400 years. My understanding of human behavior, outside the Bible, was also influenced by Dr. William M. Marston who wrote *Emotions of Normal People*, 1928, and Dr. John Geier, who originated the DISC assessment, 1972.

I discovered that the reason that we have mental, emotional, and behavioral issues isn't complicated. The solution to these issues isn't complicated either.

John T. Cocoris
McKinney, Texas

John 3:16

For God so loved the world that He gave

His only begotten Son, that whoever believes

in Him should not perish but have everlasting life.

PART I

Man's Wisdom

Chapter 1

Introduction

The Scripture is clear, there are two forms of wisdom from which we can choose to follow, that from man or that from God. James 3:13-18 (NKJV bold added):

> *Who is wise and understanding among you? Let him show by good conduct that his works are done in the meekness of wisdom. 14 But if you have bitter envy and self-seeking in your hearts, do not boast and lie against the truth. 15 **This wisdom does not descend from above, but is earthly**, sensual, demonic. 16 For where envy and self-seeking exist, confusion and every evil thing are there. 17 But the **wisdom that is from above** is first pure, then peaceable, gentle, willing to yield, full of mercy and good fruits, without partiality and without hypocrisy. 18 Now the fruit of righteousness is sown in peace by those who make peace.*

In this passage James is saying that man's wisdom produces that which is the opposite of God's wisdom. Man's wisdom leads to bitterness, envy, strife, and ***confusion***. Whereas God's wisdom produces pure motives, peace, gentleness, humility, mercy, and ***clarity***.

1

The same division is seen when trying to understand and identify the cause and cure of mental, emotional, and behavioral issues. The best that man's wisdom offers is different than God's wisdom.

This work examines the difference between what *man* has determine is the cause and cure of mental, emotional, and behavioral issues and what *God* says about these issues.

What is a Disorder?

According to the Merriam Webester dictionary, when something is labeled a "disorder" it means that something is *out of order*, or *to disturb the regular or normal functions of something.*

When it comes to mental, emotional, or behavioral issues our society has determined what it means for these three things to be *normal* or in *order*. When there is deviation from the established standard then one is said to have a *disorder*; i.e., something is *not normal.*

To establish the standard, mental health professionals began collecting what they believed was unacceptable behavior in the early 1950s. They identified symptoms that if found in a person's behavior were then labeled with a *disorder*.

Their conclusions were published in the ***Diagnostic and Statistical Manual of Mental Disorders*** referred to as the DSM-1. It has been added to since 1952 and is now called the DSM-5. The DSM-5 list the symptoms of every *disorder* determined so far.

A mental, emotional, or behavioral issue is typically labeled as a *disorder* when it meets specific criteria as outlined in the DSM-5. Mental health professionals use this manual to diagnose conditions based on symptoms, duration, and impact on daily life. For a condition to be classified as a *disorder*, in general must:

1. Cause significant distress or impairment in social, occupational, or other important areas of functioning.

2. Persist over a defined period (e.g., anxiety lasting at least six months for Generalized Anxiety Disorder).

3. Show a consistent pattern of symptoms that align with established diagnostic criteria.

4. Not be better explained by another medical condition or substance use.

The DSM-5 includes symptoms of a wide range of disorders:

1. Mood disorders

   Depression
   Bipolar

2. Anxiety disorders (the most common issue)

   Generalized anxiety disorder
   Panic disorder
   Obsessive-compulsive (OCD)
   Social anxiety disorder

3. Personality disorders

   Borderline
   Narcissistic

4. Psychotic disorders (break from reality)

   Paranoid personality
   Delusional
   Schizophrenia

5. Eating disorders

   Anorexia nervosa
   Bulimia nervosa
   Binge-eating

6. Trauma disorders

   Post-traumatic stress disorder (PTSD)
   Multiple Personalities or DID

7. Substance abuse disorders (addictions)

   Alcohol
   Drugs
   Medications

8. ADHD disorders

   Inattention
   Hyperactivity
   Impulsivity

This list is not meant to be exhaustive but only to demonstrate the kinds of mental, emotional, and behavioral issues that are labeled a "disorder," or, as some would call them a "mental illness." In my work during my internship, and at the mental hospital, and in my private practice, I have worked with all the disorders listed.

Two Treatment Options

In the mental health field, once a disorder has been determined, there are two options for intervention or treatment.

Man's wisdom, as to the cause and cure of mental, emotional, and behavioral issues, can be divided into two categories; the *non-medical* treatment and the *medical* treatment.

Non-Medical Treatment

The *non-medical* approach is made up of different ways of understanding the cause of a mental, emotional, or behavioral issue and different treatment methods *without* the use of medications.

The *SAGE Encyclopedia of Theory in Counseling and Psychotherapy* lists over 300 different approaches to counseling that do not use medication as a primary treatment option (July 29, 2019).

Some of these approaches, however, may suggest the use of medication to treat a person's symptoms. The different approaches, however, largely disagree among themselves as to what caused the problem and what to do about it.

The *non-medical* model will be addressed only briefly in the next chapter.

Medical Treatment

The *medical* approach centers around the use of medication to treat *disorders* believing that the cause is an underlying medical issue.

The *medical* model will be addressed beginning in chapter three. It is the medical model that is the main focus of man's wisdom in this book.

The *non-medical* and *medical* approaches to treating mental, emotional, and behavioral issues represent the best man's wisdom has offered.

Chapter 2

The Non-Medical Approach

The *non-medical* approach to counseling means that methods of therapy are used that do not include the primary use of medications.

Some therapists are *eclectic*. This means that a therapist will borrow different methods from several models of treatment to help a client. This may include the secondary use of medications which are used to only address the symptoms one may be having. Any use of medication must go through a person listened to write a prescription like a medical doctor or psychiatrist.

It is not practical to list all of the counseling approaches that are available (there are over 300 as mentioned). Most are not widely known or used. All of the therapeutic approaches that are commonly used and are *non-medical* can be divided into four groups as noted below:

Cognitive Therapy   Psychoanalytic
Behavioral Therapy   Humanistic

Some methods within these approaches, of course, can help people. I have used some of the techniques in counseling.

I have taken excerpts from an article entitled "Counseling Theories and Approaches," 29 July, 2023 to sum up the four groups. The article was written by Charles McAdams, Ed.D. Professor and Chair, School Psychology and Counselor Education William & Mary School of Education. (www.counseling.education.wm.edu/):

Cognitive Therapy

Cognitive counseling theories hold that people experience psychological and emotional difficulties when their thinking is out of sync with reality. When this distorted or "faulty" thinking is applied to problem solving, the result understandably leads to faulty solutions. Cognitive counselors work to challenge their clients' faulty thinking patterns so clients are able to derive solutions that accurately address the problems they are experiencing. Currently preferred cognitive-theory-based therapies include cognitive behavior therapy, reality therapy, motivational interviewing, and acceptance and commitment therapy.

Behavioral Therapy

Behavioral counseling theories hold that people engage in problematic thinking and behavior when their environment supports it. When an environment reinforces or encourages these problems, they will continue to occur. Behavioral counselors work to help clients identify the reinforcements that are supporting problematic patterns of thinking and acting and replace them with alternative reinforcements for more desirable patterns. Currently preferred therapies based in behavior theory include behavior therapy, dialectical behavior therapy, multimodal therapy and conjoint sex therapy.

Psychoanalytic

Psychoanalytic counseling theories hold that psychological problems result from the present-day influence of unconscious psychological drives or motivations stemming from past relationships and experiences. Dysfunctional thought and behavior patterns from the past have become unconscious "working models" that guide clients toward continued dysfunctional thought and behavior in their present lives. Psychoanalytic counselors strive to help their clients become aware of these unconscious working models so that their negative influence can be understood and addressed. Some currently preferred therapies grounded in psychoanalytic theory include psychoanalysis, attachment therapy, object relations therapy and Adlerian therapy.

Humanistic

Humanistic counseling theories hold that people have within themselves all the resources they need to live healthy and functional lives, and that problems occur as a result of restricted or unavailable problem-solving resources. Humanistic counselors see their role not as one of directing clients in how to address their problems but, rather, as one of helping clients to discover and access within themselves the restricted resources they need to solve problems on their own. Some currently preferred humanistic counseling therapies include person-centered, existential, emotion-focused, Gestalt and positive psychology.

For a complete and detailed treatment of major counseling approaches see my brother's book, *Counseling Theories, A Simple Explanation and Biblical Evaluation*, 2024, G. Michael Cocoris (available on Amazon and Barnes and Nobel). The following is a list of the therapeutic models he analyzes from a Biblical point of view:

Psychoanalysis	Multimodal Therapy
Analytical Psychotherapy	Existential Therapy
Psychotherapies	Person-Centered Therapy
Adlerian Psychotherapies	Gestalt Therapy
Behavioral Therapy	Transactional Analysis
Rational-Emotive Therapy	Family Therapy
Cognitive Reality Therapy	Nouthetic Counseling
Reality Therapy	

Dr. Mike Cocoris said, "From a biblical point of view, all secular psychotherapies do not include the Lord and are reductionistic in that they do not include all of the aspects of the human condition and, yet, there are biblically compatible concepts in each of them [specifically the ones noted above]."

The evaluation of the *medical* model is the main focus of man's wisdom beginning in the next chapter.

Chapter 3

The Medical Model Approach

The term *medical model* was coined by psychiatrist R. D. Laing in his *The Politics of the Family and Other Essays* (1971), for the procedures identified for which all doctors would be trained.

To explain the concept behind the medical model I have taken excerpts from an article by Lisa Fritscher entitled "Medical Model Use in Psychology." It was updated on October 30, 2023 and medically reviewed by Daniel B. Block, MD.

The Medical Model treats mental disorders as physical diseases that result in specific symptoms or functional impairments. As such, medication is often used in their treatment. The biological approach of the medical model focuses on a person's genetics, neurotransmitters, neurophysiology, neuroanatomy, and other aspects of their physical makeup. It uses the same type of framework used to diagnose and treat physical illnesses such as the common cold to also diagnose and treat psychological conditions.

The medical model teaches that issues such as anxiety, depression, bipolar, etc., have an organic or physical cause. In short, if you have a mental or emotional issue worthy of a diagnosis, it's your brain's fault, you have a chemical imbalance.

How The Brain Works

To better understand the chemical imbalance theory, it is helpful to know how the brain functions. I have included the explanation by Irving Kirsch, Ph.D., from his book, *The Emperor's New Drugs, Exploding the Antidepressant Myth*, 2011, page 82.

The human brain contains about 100 billion nerve cells called neurons. Each neuron is like an electrical wire with many branches. When a neuron fires, electrical impulses travel along its length from one end to the other. When an impulse reaches the end of a branch, it may stimulate the next neuron, influencing whether or not it fires. Neurons do not actually touch each other. Rather, there are fluid-filled gaps, called "synapse" between the end of one neuron and the beginning of another. The brain's electrical impulses are not strong enough to span these gaps. So how can a neuron's electrical impulse influence the firing of a neighboring nerve cell? It does so by means of chemicals called 'neurotransmitters', which are manufactured by neurons and convey information across the gaps between them (that is, the synapses). Serotonin is one of the neurotransmitters through which one neuron influences the firing of another. Others include norepinephrine and dopamine. There are many other kinds of neurotransmitters, but these three—and especially serotonin—have been hypothesized to be involved in depression.

After neurotransmitter molecules have influenced the firing of a receiving neuron (more technically called a postsynaptic neuron), some of them are destroyed by enzymes in the synaptic cleft (the synapse), some are reabsorbed by the sending presynaptic neuron in a process that is called 'reuptake' and the rest remain in the space between the two neurons. The chemical-imbalance hypothesis is that there is not enough serotonin, norepinephrine and/or dopamine in the synapses of the brain. This is more specifically termed the monoamine theory of depression, because both serotonin and norepinephrine belong to the class of neurotransmitters called monoamines.

The Scientific American Book of the Brain, New York: Scientific American, 1999: p. 3, states: "An adult human brain has more than 100 billion neurons." A piece of your brain, the size of a grain of sand, contains a billion of these synapses, belonging to 100,000 neurons, each of which having a unique function.

The drawing below is a depiction of the relationship between neurons and the synapse (gap).

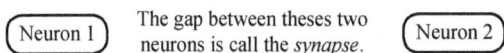

(Neuron 1) The gap between theses two (Neuron 2)
neurons is call the *synapse*.

Neurotransmitters like Serotonin, Norepinephrine, and Dopamine are used to communicate from one neuron to another. If the neurotransmitters are missing (depleted) then you are said to have a chemical imbalance.

The medical model is actually teaching that the brain is *defective*. The brain itself has stopped producing one or more chemicals that keeps you *balanced*. Once specific chemicals are depleted you become anxious, depressed, bipolar, etc. The theory further-more holds that once specific chemicals are replaced your brain returns to a *balanced* state and the issue goes away.

13

None of this has ever been proven, it's just a theory. This sounds good to some because it relieves people from being responsible for their behavior. Medical doctors (psychiatrist) believe that the *brain organ* is causing your mental and emotional problems. They teach that the *organ* of the brain has lost it's ability to function correctly—for reasons unknown.

The chemical imbalance hypothesis (theory) teaches that it is not the individual's choices, it's faulty chemistry in the brain.

Chapter 4

Origin of The Chemical Imbalance Theory

What led to the development of the chemical imbalance theory? Well, the use of drugs for all kinds of reasons is not new. Throughout all of human history drugs have been used for recreational use and to treat ailments. Sociologist Erich Goode summarizes drug use in history:

> Humans have been ingesting drugs for thousands of years. And throughout recorded time, significant numbers of nearly every society on earth have used one or more drugs to achieve certain desired physical or mental states. (https://open.lib. umn.edu/socialproblems/chapter/7-1-drug-use-in-history)

Mood altering drugs have always been available through the discovery of different plants. Anne Marie Helmenstine, Ph.D. in Biomedical Sciences, University of Tennessee at Knoxville, states:

> Long before pure chemicals were manufactured in labs, people used plants for medicine. Today, there are over 100 active ingredients derived from plants for use as drugs and medicines. (www.thoughtco.com 2- 03-2020)

Marijuana, nicotine, cocaine, heroin, morphine, aspirin, and lithium are all ingredients found in nature. Some of these have been synthesized in labs.

Lithium, for example, is a natural salt that was discovered to help people who were anxious. (It's the same ingredient used in batteries.) Medical doctors only speculate what lithium does to the body and brain—they do not know for sure.

Lithium's history stems from the Roman Empire [31 BC – AD 476] when physicians would send nervous and temperamental patients to bathe in particular bath springs in southern and eastern Europe. We now know that these particular bath springs contain the highest natural concentration of lithium salts anywhere in Europe. The drug was (re)discovered in modern times by the Australian psychiatrist John Cade in 1948. With Cade's pioneering work, lithium ushered in a new era in psychiatry: the psychopharmaco logical revolution. Its discovery predates the discoveries of the first antipsychotic and antidepressant agents, which would come ... https://www.psychologytoday.com

So, as far back as we go in history drugs have been used by mankind. It was only a matter of time before the world of medicine caught on to the idea that drugs could impact the way the brain functions. But is the use of brain drugs based on scientific facts?

The most widely accepted belief in our society is that the cause of such issues as anxiety, depression, bipolar, etc., is faulty brain chemistry. It is also regarded as the most scientific reason for mental and emotional issues. Is this true? Are there scientific facts to back up what we are being told by the medical field, specifically, psychiatrists? Just how did the chemical imbalance theory get started?

Origin of The Chemical Imbalance Theory

There is uncertainty as to how the chemical imbalance theory got its start. Here are two possibilities:

Irving Kirsch

Dr. Kirsch gave the following account of the origin of the chemical-imbalance theory in his book, *The Emperor's New Drugs, Exploding the Antidepressant Myth*, 2010, pages 83-87:

> The 1950's gave rise to the Korean War, the Cuban revolution, the Hungarian revolution, the hydrogen bomb, beatniks—and antidepressants. Two different types of *antidepressants* were developed during this decade, and in both cases the discovery of apparent antidepressant effects was serendipitous [discovered by chance].
>
> The story of how antidepressants were discovered—or perhaps 'invented" might be a better word and how they led to the development of the chemical-imbalance theory is rather convoluted. But it is worth examining, as there are important lessons to be learned from it. From the beginning, the chemical-imbalance theory was based on weak and contradictory evidence, and data contradicting it were simply ignored. This is a pattern that was to be repeated. A half-century of research has produced data indicating that the chemical-imbalance theory must be wrong. Yet it remains the most popular explanation of depression, and most of the data contradicting it continues to be ignored.

The first antidepressant was a drug called *iproniazid* that had been produced in 1951 from leftover German rocket fuel by the pharmaceutical company, Hoffinann-La Roche, and was being used for the treatment of tuberculosis. As is true of most medications, clinical trials of *iproniazid* revealed various side effects, but not all of these effects were negative. Some patients reported an increased sense of vitality and well-being. At first, this was merely considered a side effect and was ignored, but it was not long before clinicians in France and the United States began trying *iproniazid* as a treatment for depression.

In 1957, Nathan Kline, Harry Loonier and John Saunders, at the Rockland State Hospital in Orangeburg, New York, reported the first influential assessment of *iproniazid* as a *'psychic energizer'* on non-tubercular psychiatric patients, some of whom were suffering from depression.

But the study conducted by Kline and his colleagues did not include a placebo control group—placebo-controlled clinical trials had not yet become fashionable—and the antidepressant effect was assumed to be a biological response to the drug. In less than one year, more than 400,000 depressed patients had been treated with iproniazid, and the first antidepressant had been born.

One year after Kline and his colleagues reported the effect of *iproniazid* on psychiatric patients, a Swiss psychiatrist named Roland Kuhn published an article in the American Journal of Psychiatry on the antidepressant effects of the tricyclic drug *imipramine*. Like *iproniazid*, the discovery of *imipramine* as an antidepressant was accidental. Kuhn was studying the effect of *imipramine* on psychosis, not depression, but three of his patients who had been diagnosed with psychotic depression showed marked improvement, and Kuhn went on to try *imipramine* on other depressed patients. He reported that a high percentage of his patients recovered completely, usually within two to three days of being given the drug. This is quite remarkable, given the subsequent widespread belief that it takes weeks for antidepressants to take effect.

It is important to note that claims for the effectiveness of *iproniazid* and *imipramine* were not based on placebo-controlled clinical trials. Instead, they were **based on clinical impressions**. In 'discovering' the antidepressant effects of imipramine, Kuhn did not even use precise measurement, rating scales or statistics. His claim was that precise measurement led to stagnation rather than progress in medicine, and he preferred to rely on his extensive medical experience and **'artistic imagination'** instead?

It would be another decade before the chemical-imbalance theory was launched. In 1965, Joseph Schildkraut at the National Institute of Mental Health in Washington, DC, published a ground breaking paper in which he argued that depression was caused by a deficiency of the neurotransmitter norepinephrine in the gaps between neurons in the brain. Two years later Alec Coppen, a physician at West Park Hospital in Surrey, published another version of the chemical-imbalance theory. His version differed from Schildkraut's in that it put most of the blame on a different neurotransmitter, emphasizing *serotonin* rather than *norepinephrine* as the neurotransmitter that was lacking.

Here then is the logic behind the first version of the chemical-imbalance theory. *Iproniazid* is a monamine oxidase inhibitor—it inhibits the oxidation of norepinephrine and serotonin in the synapses, thereby leaving more of these neurotransmitters available in the brain. When depressed people take *iproniazid*, they get better. Therefore insufficient norepinephrine and/or serotonin causes depression.

There was a problem with this first version of the biochemical theory of depression. *Iproniazid* was not the only drug that had been reported to be effective as an antidepressant. *Imipramine*, the drug that had been tested by the Swiss psychiatrist Roland Kuhn, seemed to have similar effects. But *imipramine* is not an MAOI; it does not inhibit the destruction of neurotransmitters in the synapse. So if antidepressants worked by inhibiting monoamine oxidase, why was *imipramine* effective? How could its apparent effectiveness be reconciled with the chemical-imbalance theory?

The answer is that there are two ways in which neurotransmitter levels might be increased. One is to inhibit their destruction after they have been released into the synaptic gap. That is how MAOIs are supposed to work. Recall, however, that after a neurotransmitter is released, some of its molecules are reabsorbed by the presynaptic neuron that released them in a process that is called 'reuptake'. Blocking this reuptake process should also increase the level of neurotransmitters in the brain. In 1961, Julius Axelrod, who later received the Nobel Prize in Medicine for his work on the release and reuptake of neurotransmitters, reported that *imipramine*, as well as a few other drugs, inhibited the reuptake of norepinephrine in cats. Two years later, he reported that these drugs also inhibited the reuptake of serotonin.

The monoamine hypothesis made a good story. There is only one problem with it. It does not really fit the data. It didn't fit the data that were available in the 1960's when the theory was developed, and it does not fit the data that have accumulated since then.

20

Charly Groenendijk

Another factor in the chemical imbalance theory's beginning is reported by Charly Groenendijk on his website *www. antidepressantsfacts.com/Biochemical-Imbalance.htm*:

> In 1963, a time in U.S. psychopharmacological infancy, LIFE magazine introduced the broad public to the concept of brain chemical imbalances. Psychiatrists had been experimenting with drugs, particularly LSD, and astounding themselves at the wide variety of behaviors, emotions, and personality changes they could induce in someone with only a tiny speck of the drug. A hypothesis was born out of this. If such wide variations in behavior could be made with such a small amount of a drug, which no doubt affected the brain, then any variations from 'normal' behavior must be due to extremely fine changes in brain chemistry.

In a span of about ten years the chemical imbalance theory was accepted as fact and promoted by psychiatrists. It has been accepted as fact for over fifty years.

Dr. Kirsch goes on to offer proof that the chemical imbalance theory is incorrect. If you are going to buy one book on the chemical imbalance subject, let it be this one by Dr. Kirsch.

Any new developments?

Is there any recent research that improved our understanding of the cause of mental disorders coming from genetics or brain chemistry imbalance? No.

As we will see in the next chapter, those who represent authority in this area assert that the cause of a mental or emotional disorder is "unknown."

Chapter 5

Causes Unknown

Common issues that people face include anxiety, depression, and bipolar. Solutions are offered from therapy to medications to treat these issues. As mentioned, there are many different counseling techniques from which to choose to get help and the lists of medications that promise to relieve our symptoms are numerous.

But what causes these ailments? When mental health professionals, within the medical model, are asked what causes these problems they simply do not have an answer.

As mentioned above, in the field of counseling, *The Diagnostic and Statistical Manual of Mental Disorders, Fifth Edition* is the main reference tool that lists the symptoms of all of the so-called *disorders*. But not one time does the book list a *cause* for any disorder. The manual only lists symptoms.

On their website, the world renowned Mayo Clinic (Rochester, Minnesota) states that the cause of any disorder is *unknown*. They suggest that it may be a combination of conditions but a specific cause is *unknown*.

The following is taken directly from the Mayo Clinic website (www.https://www.mayoclinic.org/):

Causes of Anxiety?

"The causes of anxiety disorders aren't fully understood. Life experiences such as traumatic events appear to trigger anxiety disorders in people who are already prone to anxiety. Inherited traits also can be a factor.

Medical causes: For some people, anxiety may be linked to an underlying health issue. In some cases, anxiety signs and symptoms are the first indicators of a medical illness. If your doctor suspects your anxiety may have a medical cause, he or she may order tests to look for signs of a problem." Go to www.mayoclinic.org/diseases-conditions and type in "Anxiety."

Causes of Depression?

"It's not known exactly what causes depression. As with many mental disorders, a variety of factors may be involved, such as:

Biological differences. People with depression appear to have physical changes in their brains. The significance of these changes is still uncertain, but may eventually help pinpoint causes.

Brain chemistry. Neurotransmitters are naturally occurring brain chemicals that likely play a role in depression. Recent research indicates that changes in the function and effect of these neurotransmitters and how they interact with neurocircuits involved in maintaining mood stability may play a significant role in depression and its treatment.

Hormones Changes in the body's balance of hormones may be involved in causing or triggering depression. Hormone changes can result with pregnancy and during the weeks or months after delivery (postpartum) and from thyroid problems, menopause or a number of other conditions.

Inherited traits. Depression is more common in people whose blood relatives also have this condition. Researchers are trying to find genes that may be involved in causing depression." Go to www. mayoclinic.org/diseases-conditions and type in "Depression."

Causes of Bipolar?

"The exact cause of bipolar disorder is unknown, but several factors may be involved, such as:

Biological differences. People with bipolar disorder appear to have physical changes in their brains. The significance of these changes is still uncertain but may eventually help pinpoint causes.

Genetics. Bipolar disorder is more common in people who have a first-degree relative, such as a sibling or parent, with the condition. Researchers are trying to find genes that may be involved in causing bipolar disorder." Go to www.mayoclinic.org/diseases-conditions and type in "Bipolar."

Other Disorders

The well-respected Mayo Clinic states on all the diagnosis listed below that the cause is *unknown*:

Attention Deficient
Obsessive-Compulsive
Addictions
Anxiety
Depression
Narcissism
Bipolar
Borderline Personality Disorder
Schizophrenia
Psychosis

Go to *www.mayoclinic.org/diseases-conditions* and type in any of the above and you will see a message that reads like this ... "although the exact causes of [for example bipolar] behavior are not clear, possible causes may include the environment, genetics, or faulty brain chemistry."

Conclusion

Psychiatrists and psychologists are the professionals responsible for the conclusions I've noted above. Their research has determined that there are three possible contributors to explain why we have mental and emotional issues (disorders):

1. Environmental influences
2. Genetic transmission
3. Brain chemistry malfunction

The question is will these three possibilities survive close examinations? We will examine them in the next three chapters.

Chapter 6

Does The Environment Cause Behavior?

There are some that believe that the environment in which you were raised actually *causes* your behavior. This idea began with John Locke.

John Locke (1632-1704)

John Locke was an English philosopher and physician, widely regarded as one of the most influential of Enlightenment thinkers and commonly known as the "Father of Liberalism" (Wikipedia). He postulated that, at birth, the mind was a blank slate, or *tabula rasa* ... he maintained that "we are born without innate ideas, and that knowledge is instead determined only by experience derived from sense perception..."

John B. Watson (1878-1958)

John B. Watson is considered to be the "Father of Behaviorism." Behaviorists believe that the environment is the *only* determinant of behavior. They believe there is no free will and no internal roots of behavior. Behaviorists believe that behavior is conditioned completely by the environment in which a person is raised.

The Environment Does Not Cause Behavior

We would all agree that the environment in which we were raise has *some* influence on our development. But to say that the environment actually causes behavior requires one to believe that we do not possess free will—the ability to choose.

Common Sense

It's common sense to understand that babies are born with the ability to quickly make a choice. Just ask any young mother if their baby makes choices!

Theological Problem

God created Adam and Eve and they were in a perfect environment and what did they do? They made a choice to rebel against God. It was not the environment that they were in that caused their response, it was their choice *in* the environment. It was impossible for the environment to cause their rebellion!

To be clear, the environment can influence behavior either positively or negatively. However, it is always up to the individual to choose the level of influence allowed in their life.

Conclusion

There is no evidence that one's environment causes behavior. One's environment can have a positive or negative influence on behavior but that depends how one responds to their environment.

Chapter 7

Do Genes Cause Behavior?

In the field of medicine, common issues such as anxiety, depression, and bipolar (and others) are considered a *disease* justifying the label of *mental illness*. Since these issues are considered an *illness*, medical doctors are *focused on the body* to uncover the underlining cause of a disorder.

Some researchers believe that "mental illness" is somehow caused by *inherited genes*. Research Trusted Source has found that "mental illness *likely* has a genetic component, but that mental illness is **most probably caused by a combination of genetic and environmental components**. What's more, certain mental health disorders—such as bipolar disorder, schizophrenia, and depression—are more closely tied to genetics than other disorders. Studies looking at the connections between genetics and mental illness are ongoing, and there's still much to be learned."

Other researchers say, that "mental disorders are the result of both genetic and environmental factors. No single genetic switch has been found that, when flipped, causes a mental disorder. Consequently, it is difficult for doctors to determine a person's risk of inheriting a mental disorder or passing on the disorder to their children. The causes of mental disorders are complex, requiring many interacting genes and environmental factors." (www.healthychildren.org)

29

Still other researchers state, "Many mental illnesses run in families, suggesting they may be passed on from parents to children through genes. Genes contain instructions for the function of each cell in the body and are responsible for how we look, act, think, etc. However, just because your mother or father may have or had a mental illness doesn't mean you will have one. Hereditary just means that you are more likely to get the condition than if you didn't have an affected family member. Experts believe that many mental conditions are linked to problems in multiple genes—not just one, as with many diseases—which is why a person inherits a susceptibility to a mental disorder but doesn't always develop the condition. The disorder itself occurs from the interaction of these genes and other factors—such as psychological trauma and environmental stresses—which can influence, or trigger, the illness in a person who has inherited a susceptibility to it." (www.medicine.net, accessed 8-17-22)

Genes Do Not Cause Behavior

The theory is that there are "personality genes" (both good and bad) that are passed on to us that contain the markers of a mental illness and that under certain circumstances it will develop.

A favorite target of researchers is identifying the gene that produces schizophrenia. Dr. Colin Ross (psychiatrist) comments on the research on the so-called schizophrenic gene in *Pseudoscience In Biological Psychiatry: Blaming The Body*, pages 193-194, "The belief that schizophrenia is a specific organic disease or a group of organic brain diseases has never been confirmed. We have been on the verge of confirming it since the dawn of modern psychiatry [1808], and we are still on the verge."

Michael W. Kraus, Ph.D., reviewed the genetic research and published his findings in *Under the Influence* in Psychology Today, July 11, 2013. He concluded, "The current prevailing genetic evidence seems to suggest that we actually don't have genes for personality."

Conclusion

There is no evidence that inherited genes cause behavior. Behavior is determined by the choices one makes.

Chapter 8

Does A Chemical Imbalance Cause Behavior?

No. The achilles heal of the chemical imbalance theory is that it has never been scientifically proven. As previously mentioned, it is based on *clinical impressions* and *artistic imagination* instead of scientific facts.

When symptoms are reported that represent such issues as anxiety, depression, and bipolar (and others) it is *assumed* that a chemical imbalance is the cause.

However, a blood test does not exist that can reveal whether or not a neurotransmitter is depleted. A test of any kind does not exist including MRI, CAT Scan, or X-ray that shows a chemical deficit in the brain. Blood tests are given only after medication is administered to determine the levels of the drugs ingested. The chemical imbalance theory is not based on science.

An irresponsible diagnosis?

I went to my doctor years ago to get an explanation of an event that had occurred a few days earlier. Here is what happened:

I explained that I suddenly became confused and disoriented while driving. I broke out in a cold sweat, and my vision became blurry. I was unable to continue driving safely so I pulled into a parking lot. I though my blood sugar had dropped and I needed some orange juice.

Fortunately, there was a grocery store near where I had parked. It took about twenty minutes before I could gain enough control to go into the store and get sugar into my system. Still a bit disoriented, it took about ten minutes of wandering around in the store before I finally found the orange juice. I drank it quickly and then paid the clerk. I slowly regained my senses and was able to continue safely on my way.

After hearing my symptoms my doctor of ten years looked at me and said, "I have some bad news for you, you have a tumor on your pancreas!" I was stunned! My first thought was that I had cancer and I had three months to live and said to myself, "Lord I'm coming home."

He then said he wanted a second opinion and walked out of the room to phone a colleague. At that very moment my brother called. I told him that the doctor had just informed me that I had a tumor on my pancreas and that I likely had only three months to live! I said that I would call him back. I sat there lonely and numb. I had three months to live, who survives pancreatic cancer? After what seemed like hours the doctor returned to the examination room (actually about fifteen minutes). He said, "I lied, you have hypoglycemia!"

After hearing my symptoms my doctor made his diagnosis. He did not suggest scanning for a tumor on my pancreas, or giving me a glucose tolerance test, or giving me a blood test. Was he irresponsible? Many would say that he was. Medical doctors are to gather sufficient physical evidence before declaring a diagnosis—especially a potentially life-ending diagnosis.

What I experienced, of course, had nothing to do with having a chemical imbalance. It does, however, illustrate the requirement for tests to be offered before a diagnosis is determined.

Although the chemical imbalance theory is presented by medical doctors, psychologists, counselors and the media as scientific, not all agree. Here are three psychiatrists that disagree:

Dr. Colin Ross (1950 -)

Dr. Ross was my supervisor during my two year internship working with people who had Dissociative Identity Disorder (Multiple Personalities, now called DID). Dr. Ross coauthored with Alvin Pam the book, *Pseudoscience In Biological Psychiatry, Blaming The Body*, 1995. He made the following statement on page 41:

> Despite vigorous laboratory investigation, no psychiatric disorder has thus far been cured by medication, not even manic disorder where lithium treatment has been so helpful. **The efficacy of a drug does not prove that a particular mental disturbance is biochemically determined. For example, aspirin relieves headaches but no one contends that a headache is brought about by aspirin deficiency.**

Dr. Peter R. Breggin (1936 -)

Dr. Breggin is probably the most outspoken critic of the chemical imbalance theory. He has written two books on this subject: *Toxic Psychiatry*, 1991; he coauthored with David Cohen, *Your Drug May Be Your Problem, How and Why to Stop Taking Psychiatric Medications*, 1999. Dr. Breggin draws this conclusion in *Toxic*

Psychiatry, page 171:

> Since the antidepressants frequently make people feel worse, since they interfere with both psychotherapy and spontaneous improvement by blunting the emotions and confusing the mind, since most are easy tools for suicide, since they have many adverse physical side effects, since they can be difficult to withdraw from, and since there's little evidence for their effectiveness—it makes sense never to use them.

Dr. Peter Breggin states in *Your Drug May Be your Problem: How and Why To Stop Taking Psychiatric Medications*, page 12:

> Psychiatric medications are, first and foremost, psychoactive or psychotropic drugs. They influence the way a person feels, thinks, and acts. Like cocaine and heroin, they change the emotional response capacity of the brain. If used to solve emotional problems, they end up shoving those problems under the rug of drug intoxication while creating additional drug-induced problems.

Dr. Breggin was interviewed by The Epoch Times (date unknown) and said the following:

> Zoloft, Prozac, and Paxil are classified as selective serotonin reuptake inhibitors (SSRIs). Doctors have made unsubstantiated claims that the inhibition of reuptake of serotonin alleviates depression. As neurotransmitters carry messages between nerves, the reuptake mechanism returns some of them to the nerves where they were created increasing serotonin in the synapses. This is the explanation

psychiatrists give patients but many scientists have long doubted the overly simple explanation that serotonin could be responsible for depression, sadness, apathy, and other things linked to depression. Serotonin is the most widespread neurotransmitter throughout the brain, so it affects all kinds of things. It is in the gut [from where it originated], it is in the bloodstream, so this idea is ridiculous.

Low serotonin is claimed to be the cause of depression and referred to as if it's only in the brain. Actually it has many functions and it is all over the body. Serotonin is a chemical that carries messages between nerve cells in the brain and throughout your body. Serotonin plays a key role in such body functions as mood, sleep, digestion, nausea, wound healing, bone health, blood clotting and sexual desire. Serotonin levels that are too low or too high can cause physical and psychological health problems. (https://my.clevelandclinic.org/health/articles/22572-serotonin)

Dr. William Glasser (1925-2013)

Dr. Glasser states the following in his book, *Warning: Psychiatry Can Be Hazardous to Your Mental Health*, 2003, pages xii-xiii:

The medical approach to mental distress is based on an unproven hypotheses, in particular the theory that the fundamental cause of mental distress is biological, either a biochemical imbalance, a genetic defect, or both. Psychiatry has convinced itself and the general public that this hypothesis is not a hypothesis but a proven fact. In doing so, modem psychiatry has made a major error of judgment, an error so fundamental that it should never occur in any discipline purporting to be scientific. But psychiatry gets away with it, because instead of policing psychiatry to ensure that it does not lose the run of itself, legislators and the general public alike place great faith and trust in the integrity and objectivity of psychiatry and psychiatric research. What limited policing there is of psychiatry is not in-depth and relies heavily on the bonafides of psychiatrists and medical researchers.

Here's the latest

Hilary Brueck published a report about Dr. Mark Horowitz experience and research on October 7, 2022. (https://www.yahoo.com/video/psychiatry-professor-taught-students-depression-110000707.html) Here are excerpts from that article:

> When Mark Horowitz was 21, he began taking antidepressants. At the time, he was feeling a "bit miserable" in school—like "a neurotic, Woody Allen kind of guy." His medical provider suggested he start taking a selective serotonin reuptake inhibitor, or SSRI. He never imagined the debilitating withdrawal symptoms he'd experience 13 years later while trying to come off the drug.
>
> Today, 19 years after he began, Horowitz is determined to stop taking his SSRI for good. He's slowly, methodically undertaking what may be a years long process to wean himself off the drug, using a liquid version and decreasing his dose by just a smidgen every few weeks to avoid panic attacks. Horowitz isn't just any patient, though. He's the psychiatry researcher behind a major new study showing that there's no solid link between low serotonin levels and depression.
>
> Based on his research, Horowitz believes SSRIs like Lexapro aren't really doing what he was once led to

believe: correcting a "chemical imbalance" in his brain. In fact, he says it's high time that this conventional wisdom is properly debunked for the general public once and for all, instead of being relegated to watercooler chatter among academics, doctors, and drugmakers.

Almost seven years after finishing his Ph.D., Horowitz said he still hasn't found any compelling evidence. His latest analysis, released in the journal Molecular Psychiatry in July [2022], is yet another review of serotonin research through the years and concludes that there is no solid link between low serotonin levels and depression.

But after years of hearing otherwise from pharmaceutical companies on TV and general practitioners with just minutes to spare for a clinic visit and a prescription refill, it can be alarming to learn that these first-line, top-selling depression drugs—taken by upward of one in five American adults every year, according to recent estimates—don't reliably work. The truth is that scientists still don't really understand how they do what they do.

Horowitz has another theory. In studies, roughly half of patients taking antidepressants like SSRIs report a numbing or dulling of their emotions while on the drugs. If antidepressants are changing the chemistry of our brains, thereby producing changes to our thoughts and emotions, maybe they are simply blunting emotional pain.

Horowitz has another theory. In studies, roughly half of patients taking antidepressants like SSRIs report a numbing or dulling of their emotions while on the drugs. If antidepressants are changing the chemistry of our brains, thereby producing changes to our thoughts and emotions, maybe they are simply blunting emotional pain. "People become depressed because they get into difficulties in life," Horowitz said. Maybe SSRIs work by effectively interrupting those painful thoughts.

Unfortunately, such numbing isn't confined to negative emotions. Antidepressant drugs can also alter patients' sex drives and increase suicidal thoughts, particularly among young people. It's still not well-understood why that happens.

Conclusion

Although the chemical imbalance theory is presented as scientific it is void of scientific facts. Medical doctors do not have a blood test of any kind to establish a chemical imbalance in the brain.

"Decades of intensive psychiatric research have failed to establish a biological cause for any psychiatric condition."

Dr. William Glasser

Chapter 9

But The Drugs Helped Me!

When discussing this issue with patients that are on medications I have been asked, "How do you explain that the medications helped me calm down?"

I have established that these medications have not been proven to do what is claimed; restore the chemicals that the brain is not producing. How then do we explain the change in people taking these medications?

Tranquilizers blunt the emotions

I worked at a mental hospital where we were required to give to each patient a list of the medications that were being used—one or more of which would be administered to them. This list included all of the current medications on the market.

The entire list of medications was called "Tranquilizers." A tranquilizer is a calming drug. It's a medication that will blunt emotions from being expressed. The truth is that if you give any kind of tranquilizer to one who is emotional, anxious, depressed or upset they will calm down and feel better.

Being human is possessing the capability of controlling your thoughts, emotions, and behavior. Some choose to and others do not.

If you are routinely emotional over most anything, you can choose not to be. You take a pill, you feel better—the medication did for you what you chose not to do for yourself, so...

Medication will do for you
what you will not do for yourself.

Now, granted, some upsetting events make it more difficult to calm yourself—a traumatic event often requires more time to adjust. I am not referring to events that all would recognize as appropriate. Significant loss requires time to adjust.

Some people routinely get upset over little things and are anxious and emotional. Sometimes emotions fluctuate widely up and down. These people depend on medication to keep them level when they could do it themselves by applying coping skills.

Placebo Effect

We cannot rule out the placebo effect which means that one has a positive response just because they took a pill and not because of what the pill actually did.

Most everyone has heard of an experiment that has been conducted whereby a "sugar pill" was given to someone to see if they reported a positive response believing that it was medication.

The Efficacy of a Drug

Remember Dr. Ross' comment; "The efficacy of a drug does not prove that a particular mental disturbance is biochemically determined.

For example, aspirin relieves headaches but no one contends that a headache is brought about by aspirin deficiency."

Drugs manage symptoms only

All the psych drugs do is address the symptoms that one is having, they do not repair or fix anything.

Conclusion

All psych drugs fall under the larger category of tranquilizers. The main effect is they blunt the emotions from being expressed. There is no scientific proof that psych meds do what they are advertised to do.

Chapter 10

Side Effects of Psychiatric Drugs

There are side-effects with any medication you take including aspirin. All psychotropic medications will have mild to severe side effects. The seriousness of which depends on the specific medication, the dosage, the medical condition of the one ingesting the drug, and other drugs being used. Not all drugs affect people the same.

The websites, *www.drugs.com* and *www.healthline.com*, offer information on the use of theses medications and side effects.

I've listed four major categories and the drugs frequently used for each. As you will see, some medications are used for more than one diagnosis. Also, some of the medications share some of the same side effects. Be aware that any medication you take will spread throughout your body.

The purpose of this section is to make you aware of the side effects of the various medications. If you are taking psych meds please read carefully the instructions that come with each prescription.

1. Anti-depressants. Not everyone experiences significant side effects with antidepressants.

Common medications used:
Fluoxetine (Prozac)   Citalopram (Celexa)
Sertraline (Zoloft)   Paroxetine (Paxil)
Escitalopram (Lexapro)

Common side effects:
Tremors
Drowsiness, dizziness
Hair thinning
Lithium toxicity (can cause confusion, tremors,
    seizures, and kidney damage
Liver damage
Blood disorders (low platelets or white blood cell count)
Nausea
Fatigue or insomnia
Sexual dysfunction (reduced libido)
Weight gain or loss
Dry mouth
Anxiety or restlessness
Suicidal thoughts or behavior, (young adults)

3. **Anti-anxiety** (Benzodiazepines are minor tranquilizers)

Common medications used:
Xanax   Librium   Ativan
Klonopin   Valium

Common side effects:
Memory problems   Lack of coordination
Slurred speech   Cognitive impairment
Drowsiness, dizziness or lightheadedness
Risk of overdose when combined with alcohol
    and depressants

4. Antipsychotics. The following meds are commonly used to address delusions, hallucinations, and confused thinking and speaking.

Common medications used:

Thorazine	Abilify	Risperdal
Haldol	Prolixin	
Seroquel	Zyprexa	

Common side effects:

Drowsiness or sedation
Weight gain
Increased appetite
Dry mouth
Constipation
Blurry vision
Tardive dyskinesia (involuntary, repetitive body movements)
Neuroleptic malignant syndrome (a rare but life-threatening condition causing muscle rigidity, fever, and altered mental status)
Increased risk of metabolic issues (like diabetes and high cholesterol)
Cardiovascular issues (e.g., arrhythmias)

What are the ingredients in psychiatric drugs?

The chemical makeup of almost all psychiatric drug is nearly 100% synthetic. Since most all these drugs are not from natural ingredients it may be sufficient to explain why there are some severe reactions.

Synthetic vs. natural. Most prescription psychiatric drugs (like antidepressants, anti psychotics, mood stabilizers, and anxiolytics) are fully synthetic chemicals—made in labs from non-biological starting materials. Examples:

SSRIs (e.g., fluoxetine/Prozac, sertraline/Zoloft)
Antipsychotics (e.g., risperidone, olanzapine)
Mood stabilizers (e.g., lamotrigine)

These are chemically synthesized and do not contain any natural or plant-derived components.

Exceptions. Some drugs were originally derived from natural sources but are now synthesized for consistency and cost:

Lithium (a naturally occurring element) is still used as lithium carbonate, not synthetic in origin.
Opioid-related psychiatric medications (e.g., methadone) may be semi-synthetic.

Supplements or plant-based compounds like St. John's Wort (a natural antidepressant) are rarely used.

Conclusion: All psych medications have side effects from mild to severe. It's crucial for an individual taking psychotropic medications to communicate openly with their healthcare provider about any side effects experienced.

Abruptly stopping certain medications can lead to withdrawal symptoms or a recurrence of symptoms. It's important to follow the prescribed treatment plan and consult with a healthcare provider before making any changes. Regular monitoring and follow-up appointments are essential to address concerns.

Chapter 11

An Errant Path

Psychiatry (the medical model) has gone too far trying to explain behavior that they have decided is outside the acceptable norm in our society. Actually, acceptable behavior is being reduced by the *frequent additions* of new diagnosis in the DSM revisions.

To illustrate how absurd it has become they are now attempting to call ordinary daydreaming and mind-wandering in children as a disorder called sluggish cognitive tempo (SCT)! The following excerpt is from an article by Alan Schwartz that was published in the New York Times newspaper April 11, 2014; "Idea of New Attention Disorder Spurs Research, and Debate."

> Yet now some powerful figures in mental health are claiming to have identified a new disorder that could vastly expand the ranks of young people treated for attention problems. Called sluggish cognitive tempo, the condition is said to be characterized by lethargy, daydreaming and slow mental processing. By some researchers' estimates, it is present in perhaps two million children."
>
> "I have no doubt there are kids who meet the criteria for this thing, but nothing is more irrelevant," Dr. Frances said. "The enthusiasts here are thinking of missed patients. What about the mislabeled kids who are called patients when there's nothing wrong with them? They are not considering what is happening in the real world.

The real world is made up of parents that recognize that children are born with different personalities or natural tendencies (temperament). Some are extroverts and some are introverts. Some children are easy to raise and others are not. Extroverts are easily distracted and they need lots of activity. Introverts adapt to their environment not wanting to be disruptive.

There are common sense reasons why children daydream or their mind drifts around while in a classroom. They could just be bored or not interested in the subject. They just might have a boring teacher.

If we continue down this path that modern psychiatry is leading us we will soon loose the ability to identify what is normal behavior. As of the printing of this book (2025) SCT is not listed in the DSM.

In 1969 the song "In The Year 2525" written by Richard Lee Evans was number one for six weeks. Here are the opening words of the song sung by Zager and Evans:

In the year 2525,
If man is still alive,
If woman can survive,
They may find-
In the year 3535
Ain't gonna need to tell the truth,
Tell no lies.
Everything you think, do, and say
Is in the pill you took today.

These words were written in 1969 and were not meant to be prophetic but over 50 years later look where we are headed. The following illustrations shows just how far our society has gone to excuse behavior because of the influence of psychiatry.

The incident happened near Fort Worth, Texas in June, 2013. A sixteen year old boy acknowledged that he was drunk on alcohol and Valium when he lost control of his speeding pickup truck and slammed into a broken-down car, killing four people.

His attorneys claimed he had been spoiled by his parents and was never taught right from wrong or a sense of responsibility; a term one witness dubbed "affluenza." He was sentenced to 10 years' probation. No jail time. This is an inconceivable conclusion because it removes the boy from the consequences of the choices he willfully made.

This is the result of psychiatry promoting that behavior is determined by something other than the individual making choices. In their view no one is actually responsible for their own behavior since genetics, and faulty brain chemistry contribute to or cause behavior.

The above case illustrates that if you are not raised appropriately then you are not accountable for your choices. As a result, absurd, irresponsible, and mind numbing statements are made like mental illnesses are not the result of personal weakness, lack of character, or poor upbringing.

Summary. Psychiatry, using the medical model, is leading us down the wrong path. The two areas identified as causing or contributing to so-called mental disorders do not survive close investigation.

The genetic connection has not been established and the chemical imbalance theory cannot be proven scientifically.

The field of psychiatry has labeled common and ordinary sadness over a loss as depression and medication is offered. Hyperactive children are labeled ADD or ADHD and medicated. Natural shyness is labeled as a social phobia. Severe mood shifts are explained as a chemical imbalance in the brain and given the label of bipolar. Typical anxiety is also identified as a condition requiring medication.

There has been a hostile takeover by psychiatry for behavior that can be explained another way other than by genetics and a chemical imbalance.

Chapter 12

Summary of Man's Wisdom

I divided *Man's Wisdom* into two categories; the *non-medical* and the *medical* approach to identifying and treating mental and emotional issues. Here is a summary of the problems with man's wisdom.

Leaves God out

The nonmedical approach includes over 300 different models. Some include biblically compatibility methods but basically excluded God or the Bible from the solution to a person's problem.

No scientific facts

The medical model approach is only a theory which has never been proven. Actually, there is no scientific evidence to support the theory that people can have a chemical imbalance in the brain.

The early pioneers used *clinical impressions* and *artistic imagination* to arrive at the conclusion that there is such a thing as a chemical imbalance not clinically proven facts.

No blood test

There is no known blood test that can be used to determine *if* there is a chemical imbalance. It's theorized by the medical doctor, psychiatrists, or mental health professional that your symptoms are suggesting that your brain chemistry is *out of balance*.

I've never seen anything written on what brain chemistry balance is because no one knows! Using their logic then, the absence of extremes mentally and emotionally would suggest your brain chemistry is in balance.

No known cause

The medical model (DSM-5) fails to identify the cause of mental and emotional issues. The Mayo Clinic states for each so-called disorder that the cause is "unknown." They add that the cause is probably related to environmental influences, genetics, or faulty brain chemistry.

Conclusion

If you accept that the organ of the brain is at fault for mental or emotional issues due to a chemical imbalance you are ignoring the facts. It's a theory that has never been proven. There is no blood test used to determine the balance or imbalance of the brain's chemistry.

The medications used have a "tranquilizing" effect on the brain and body, that's all, they do not fix anything. Any tranquilizer will calm a person.

Actually, this theory is saying that your brain is faulty, it is not producing chemicals that you need to stay "balanced."

The medical model essentially teaches that anyone who develops a mental or emotional issue has been *victimized* by their body. It's not your fault, your body has betrayed you.

The medical model and it's theory of chemical imbalance is only a theory, it is presented, however, as scientific fact. Actually it's a lie. A chemical imbalance doesn't exist until one takes a psych med, now they have a chemical imbalance! The very thing they claim to fix, they actually cause! The Biblical term for promoting such a lie as this is called *deception*.

PART II

Normal, Natural
Behavior

Chapter 13

What Is Normal Behavior?

In order to understand the concept underlying the chemical imbalance theory it is necessary to first define *normal behavior*. Wikipedia (the on-line free Encyclopedia) offers this definition of *normal*:

> In behavior, normal refers to a lack of significant deviation from the average. The phrase *not normal* is often applied in a negative sense (asserting that someone or some situation is improper, sick, etc.) Abnormality varies greatly in how pleasant or unpleasant this is for other people.

The Oxford English Dictionary defines *normal* as "conforming to a standard." Another possible definition is that *normal* is someone who conforms to the predominant behavior in a society. This can be for any number of reasons such as simple imitative behavior, deliberate or inconsistent acceptance of society's standards, fear of humiliation or rejection, etc.

The French sociologist Émile Durkheim indicated in his *Rules Of The Sociological Method* that *the most common behavior in a society is considered normal.* People who do not go along are violating social norms and will invite a sanction, which may be positive or negative, from others in the society."

So, normal behavior is that which does not deviate far from the accepted behavior established by a society.

Labels and Medication

Our society does not know what to do with behavior that is outside of the accepted social norm. I am not talking about illegal or immoral behavior that would be unacceptable in any civilized society. Nor I am speaking about hormonal changes that can altar moods that women typically experience. I am specifically speaking about anxiety, depression, bipolar, schizophrenia, and other diagnosis which are common labels used today for so-called *mental illness*. Notice the diagram below:

Deviation from the norm = label/medication

Normal, Acceptable Behavior

Deviation from the norm = label/medication

When our society encounters behavior that is either above or below that which is accepted as "normal" it is labeled or medicated. For example, when someone is experiencing sadness with changes in eating, sleeping, etc, they are likely to be labeled as "depressed" and then medicated to treat the so-called *mental illness*. There is a reason that people get "depressed" as I will discuss later. The same is true of the so-called bipolar disorder. These are people that have either extreme highs or extreme lows (or both) as well as other symptoms. There is a reason that people behave this way as I will discuss later. Medical science labels and medicates that which they do not understand, that which deviates from what has been accepted as normal behavior. Their position is that an imbalance in brain chemistry causes abnormal or extreme behavior.

If the chemical imbalance theory is not correct then there must be another way of explaining the behaviors mentioned. I believe there is.

Chapter 14

Natural Behavior is Normal

Natural behavior is God's design.

You know others to be extroverts, or introverts, some smile a lot and others do not. You know people that are socially active and others that are not. We think of such people as just "being themselves." These activities represent natural, normal behavior. That people are born with *natural* tendencies is not a new idea, it's been around for thousands of years.

Four Temperaments

There are four categories of *natural* behavior referred to as *four temperaments*. Hippocrates (470?-360? B.C.) is credited with originated the concept but it is known to have existed long before. The concept was further developed by Galen (129-216 AD). The four categories of natural behavior are; Choleric, Sanguine, Phlegmatic, and Melancholy.

A person's **temperament represents behavior that is natural, normal, and *absent of extremes*.** It is behavior, that you have observed, and now expect, from people that you have known for a some time. Dr. William Moulton Marston wrote in *Emotions of Normal People*, 1928, p. 2:

I do not regard you as a "normal person" emotionally, when you are suffering from fear, rage, pain, shock, desire to deceive, or any other emotional state whatsoever containing turmoil and conflict. Your emotional responses are *normal* when they produce pleasantness and harmony.

Dr. Marston regarded behavior to be natural and normal as long as it did not display an extreme expression of emotions.

Character Temperament is *not* the same as *character* nor is it the same as *personality*. Temperament is part of one's personality. Temperament has nothing to do with your level of maturity.

Traits Temperament represents a **cluster** of **inborn traits**. A trait can be possessed from low to high which means you can possess a lot of a trait or a little of the same trait.

Drive Temperament is a **drive** or **force** within that **urges** certain behavior. Temperament is an **appetite** that requires satisfaction.

Need Temperament is a **need**. The drive (motivation to act) of the various temperaments is based on *natural needs* of a specific temperament blend. These **needs** drive or urge a person to behave in a manner that represents their particular temperament. Each temperament has specific needs that are different from the other temperaments. A need, according to Abraham Maslow, is something that if you do not have, you get sick. This is true in three specific areas:

1. *Physically*, people become ill without air, food, water, etc.
2. *Emotionally*, people become ill without love, affection, security, etc.
3. *Temperamentally*, if your natural needs are not met, you

will become frustrated, angry, irritable, even depressed. This may actually cause you to become emotionally and physically ill.

Your temperament represents such dominant needs that it cannot be *hidden* (your normal, daily, demeanor will represent your *natural* tendencies). On occasion you may *temporarily* behave differently as the need arises.

Your temperament needs cannot be *denied,* your temperament will actually *require* you to behave in a manner that represents your *natural* tendencies most of the time.

So, the natural tendencies with which you were born (temperament blend) will represent how you behave *most* of the time.

For a more detailed treatment of the four temperaments see my book, *Why We Do What We Do; New Insights Into The Temperament Model of Behavior*, John Cocoris, 2020. This book is a revision of my book, *The Temperament Model of Behavior; Born With Natural Tendencies*, John Cocoris, 2009.

The four temperaments are combined into 12 blends as follows:

Choleric-Sanguine	Sanguine-Choleric
Choleric-Phlegmatic	Sanguine-Phlegmatic
Choleric-Melancholy	Sanguine-Melancholy
Phlegmatic-Choleric	Melancholy-Choleric
Phlegmatic-Sanguine	Melancholy-Sanguine
Phlegmatic-Melancholy	Melancholy-Phlegmatic

Extrovert

CHOLERIC	**SANGUINE**
Result-Oriented D Style (Dominant) Command in voice Confident	People-Oriented I Style (Inducement) Expressive Friendly
Brief, Direct, To The point	Talkative, Impulsive, Playful
Asks: "What?" 10% of population	Asks: "Who?" 35% of population
Positive Outlook	Positive Outlook
PHLEGMATIC	**MELANCHOLY**
Service-Oriented S Style (Steadiness) Accommodating Loyal	Detailed-Oriented C Style (Compliant) Analytical Cautious
Routine, Non-emotional, Non-assertive	Likes to plan, Private, Organized
Asks: "How?" 25% of population	Asks: "Why?" 30% of population
Passive Outlook	Negative Outlook

Task
People

People
Task

Introvert

Everyone is a combination of all four temperaments. The first and second temperaments combine the tendencies of each temperament to produce behavior that represents both temperaments. The second temperament will modify the expression of the first temperament. For example:

Choleric-Sanguine This person is driven to get results quickly and they have some social interactions with friends. Their friends are usually chosen to help them get results.

Choleric-Phlegmatic This person is driven to get results quickly. They prefer to work alone. They have a stoic expression and can be very blunt when communicating. They need alone time to rest. This blend is extremely rare.

Choleric-Melancholy This person is driven to get results quickly with a well thought through plan. They need alone time to think and plan.

68

Sanguine-Choleric This person has boundless energy. They are very active and they are always around people. They know lots of people but they do not know them well. They are impulsive and avoid details.

Sanguine-Phlegmatic This person is relationship driven. They make lots of friends and keep them sometimes for their entire lifespan. They need time alone to rest.

Sanguine-Melancholy This person is the most creative of the twelve blends. They need social contact with others and time alone to think and plan. They have natural mood shifts.

Phlegmatic-Choleric They are very private people that have a strong determination and drive to accomplish a task and maintain a routine. This is a very rare combination.

Phlegmatic-Sanguine This is a routine person that needs some social contact. They are family oriented. They tend to talk a lot.

Phlegmatic-Melancholy This person is routine, private, and very family oriented. They tend to keep the same job and will change very little over their lifespan.

Melancholy-Choleric This person can be a perfectionist. They tend to push to achieve what they believe in. They tend to have a few close friends. They operate from a plan.

Melancholy-Sanguine This person enjoys some social involvement with family and close friends. They tend to talk a lot. They are easy to be around and they operate from a plan. They need alone time.

Melancholy-Phlegmatic This is a private person that follows a routine. They have a few close friends and enjoys privacy. They are driven to figure out what is *right* (they are not trying to be right).

Important Note

It is critical to understanding the temperament concept to know the following three principles. This will explain the reason that two people can have the same temperament blend and express it differently.

1. *Proximity* refers to the distance between the *primary* and *secondary* temperament. The proximity is fixed and will not change throughout a person's lifespan.

The *closer* the *second* temperament is to the *primary* temperament, the *less* you see of the *primary* temperament tendencies in behavior and more of the *secondary* tendencies will be visible.

The *further* the *second* temperament is from the *primary* temperament, *more* of the *primary* temperament tendencies are visible in behavior and less of the secondary temperament tendencies will be visible. The primary temperament will be more *intensely* expressed the greater the separation from the second temperament.

2. *Position* refers to the *order* of the third and fourth temperaments. This alignment *may* or *may not* have significant influence on how the *primary* and *secondary* temperament combination is expressed in behavior.

However, significant influence is observed because a temperament is *last*, indicating the lack of tendencies of that temperament. When the Choleric temperament is *third* it does make a significant difference in behavior.

70

3. *Intensity* refers to the degree to which a temperament is expressed in behavior. The expression can be from slight, to intense, to being overwhelming.

Conclusion

A person's temperament represents natural and therefore normal behavior.

Some temperament blends are naturally result-oriented and others are not. Some temperament blends are naturally socially active and others are not. Some temperament blends are naturally emotionally steady and others are not. Some temperament blends are naturally detailed oriented and others are not. Some temperament blends are naturally non-emotional and routine and others are not.

How the temperament view of behavior applies to psychology and counseling is in the next section.

PART III

Temperaments, Psychology, & Counseling

Chapter 15

Psychology & Temperaments

Much of this chapter first appeared in my book *The Temperament Model of Behavior, Born With Natural Tendencies*, 2009.

Wilhelm Wundt (1832-1920) is considered the father of modern psychology. He separated psychology from philosophy to establish it as a separate discipline in 1879.

Although the four temperament concept has been around for thousands of years it was given superficial mention at best after the new field of psychology was established. The subject is either not mentioned, mentioned a little, or written off as being too old or irrelevant. The authors of *Introduction To Psychology and Counseling, Christian Perspectives and Applications* (Meier, Minirth, Wicher, and Ratcliff, page 225, 1994) made this statement:

> While there are a number of theories of personality, four have been dominant in this century. One of the oldest theories of personality is the *trait* theory. The ancient Greeks categorized people as phlegmatic (emotionless), choleric (active and irritable), sanguine (happy), and melancholic (depressive). LaHaye (1971) attempted to incorporate these temperaments into a Christian framework, but most psychologists would agree that these categories are hopelessly dated.

Tim LaHaye writes in *Understanding The Male Temperament, What Every Man Would Like to Tell His Wife About Himself...But Won't*, 1977, "Even the psychologists who have attended my Family Life Seminars, if not hostile, appeared totally uninformed on the subject."

I completed a degree in counseling and doctorate in psychology and the four temperaments where mentioned briefly in one small paragraph in a book on psychology. So, I can report that nothing has changed since LaHaye make his comments in 1977. The most revealing, useful, and helpful model of human behavior has simply been disregarded and relegated to obscurity.

Nature verses Nurture

Perhaps the reason for not giving the temperament model of behavior serious consideration is because of a major debate in psychology over which has the most influence on behavior, *nature* or *nurture*.

Is it what you are born with (*nature*) or your interaction with the environment into which you are born (*nurture*)? Are you born with traits and tendencies or were you born with nothing (blank) and everything comes from experience and the interaction with your environment? Which is it? This debate concerns the relative importance of an individual's innate qualities (*nature*) versus influence and personal experiences (*nurture*) in determining or causing behavior patterns, and individual differences in personality.

The *nature* position, also referred to as *nativism*, is the view that certain skills or abilities are *native* or hard-wired into the brain prior to birth.

The *nurture* position is that humans acquire all or almost all of their behavioral tendencies after birth and is referred to as *tabula rasa* (i.e., born as a blank slate). Sir Francis Galton (1822–1911) wrote about distinguishing between the greater influence of heredity (*nature*) and environment (*nurture*) and coined these two terms.

The *nature* position supports the temperament model of behavior which teaches that an individual is born with *traits* or natural tendencies: people are born predisposed (hard-wired) to a way of thinking, feeling, and behaving. With pre-wired tendencies, the *nature* position holds that a person's personality is not determined by the environment. Rather, the individual responds to their environment based on their pre-wired temperament tendencies and develops their strengths and weaknesses (or not) accordingly. It follows, therefore, that an individual makes choices based on their predisposed way of thinking, feeling, and behaving. This is the temperament model of behavior.

The field of psychology holds almost exclusively to the *nurture* position believing that environmental influences have the greater impact in determining a person's personality and behavior. *Nature* is recognized as having only slight, if any, influence by some psychologists.

All would agree that *nurture* is vitally important in the early environment of a child and can have great impact. However, just because a person was raised in a good environment or a bad environment does not guarantee that the person will follow their respective example, good or bad. My opinion is that the *nurture* position places too much emphasis on the environment in which the person is raised. It relieves and/or reduces the accountability and responsibility of the individual for the choices they make. This position makes it easy for people to blame others for their own behavior: "I am this way because my mother, father, brother, sister, aunt, uncle, friend, neighbor, dog, or cat did this or that to me!" The age in which we live encourages blaming everything and everyone else for one's bad behavior *but* the one behaving badly.

A basic, but overlooked, truth is that an individual makes choices in the environment in which they are raised. I have counseled people who have come from good environments and rebelled against their training. Likewise, I have counseled people who came from bad environments and decided not to follow the examples they were shown. We easily forget that human beings make their own choices, even as a child. My conclusion is that it is not the environment that is most important, it is the person's *response* to their environment. I am not suggesting that a caregiver's bad example is to be excused or minimized.

Summary. The temperament model of behavior teaches that people are born with natural tendencies. These natural tendencies are in the *core* of an individual representing natural drives and needs. An individual is born with their temperament already determined (hard-wired). The individual then responds to their environment according to their temperament drives and needs. Temperament is, therefore, the platform upon which an individual responds to people and events.

This model teaches that we are responsible to use the associated strengths of our temperament, and overcome the natural weaknesses in order to live an effective and productive life. It's a choice.

This author agrees with Dr. Tim LaHaye that those within the field of psychology are either uninformed, misinformed, or hostile toward this concept. I must add that those who are opposed to the temperament concept do not offer research to refute the existence or importance of the four temperaments, they just deny its relevance.

Chapter 16

Counseling & Temperaments

Since the field of psychology rejects the relevance of the four temperaments, it is of no surprise that the temperament model of behavior in counseling is also entirely ignored.

Schools of Psychotherapy

As mentioned earlier, there are over 300 different schools of psychotherapy, however, there are only 15 modalities that are commonly used by therapists. Only Carl Jung embraced the concept of the temperaments to explain behavior. It is, however, only touched on slightly and not given serious consideration. Some therapists do use the temperament model on some level but there is no major methodology in psychology or counseling that seriously considers this approach to explain behavior. When the concept is used it is mostly through *The Myers-Briggs Type Indicator*. This instrument is not without controversy.

Using The Temperament Model of Behavior

The temperament model of behavior teaches that everyone is born with natural tendencies which determines their level of emotion, speed of response, and natural approach to people and events. As noted earlier, this understanding has been around for at least 2,400 years, enduring the test of time.

The temperament model of behavior is the best tool I have used in my counseling practice. To make the tool more useful, I developed the *DISC Strengths Temperament Assessment* which identifies a person's natural temperament and blend. Once I have validated the temperament blend and pattern with the client, I know the following:

Natural strengths and weaknesses
Natural temperament needs
Natural core drives
Natural fears
Method of thinking and reasoning
Potential causes of stress and anxiety
Typical **responses to pressure and stress**
Potential areas of relationship conflicts
Causes of depression
Approach to accomplishing a task
Cause of procrastination
The traits needed for balance
The reason for mood shifts and wide swings
The keys to relating to them effectively...and more.

Knowing these things listed above gives a therapist more insight into how a client thinks and processes information. It enables a therapist to understand the core drives of the one they are trying to help. Another benefit of using the temperament model of behavior in counseling is that after validating a client's temperament pattern, the client easily opens up about personal issues. They trust quickly because they see that I really do understand them.

Another benefit in using the temperament model of behavior in counseling is that the message to clients is that they are *normal*. Many people go through life comparing themselves to people they admire or envy and believe that they are inferior. It is easy for them to believe that others are *normal* but they are not.

When the client is able to see themselves in the context of the four temperaments, and identify with others with the same blend, they have a sense of belonging—they are not alone. It is a comfort and relieving to find out that there are others that think and feel the same way they do and that they are exactly the person they were designed and need to be!

The information the *DISC Strengths Temperament Assessment* opens up many areas of discussion that may not have otherwise been possible. Clients will benefit beyond the reason that brought them to counseling.

Temperaments: Who Comes To Counseling And Why

I began developing and using the four temperament concept in 1977. I worked in a mental hospital for three years and I had a private counseling practice for twenty-five years. Here is what I've learned about people with certain temperament blends who seek counseling.

First, anyone, regardless of their temperament blend, can and has sought help in counseling. No one is immured from needing help to understand and navigate an issue in their life.

Some people with certain temperament blends seek counseling rarely. Other people with different temperament blends seek counseling more often. And then one person with a specific temperament blend seeks counseling the most as will be discussed. I've arranged the following temperaments in the order they seek counseling from the least to the most.

Choleric

The three Choleric blends are Choleric-Sanguine, Choleric-Phlegmatic, and Choleric-Melancholy. People with any of the Choleric blends rarely seek counseling because they are so self-confident and possess natural problem-solving skills. In my years of counseling I remember briefly seeing three. I did not encounter one Choleric while working at the mental hospital. The Choleric blends are the least of all the temperament blends and a female Choleric is extremely rare.

The core drive of the Choleric blends is to overcome opposition to get quick results. They are self-confident and forceful to get results of any kind. They are by nature not compassionate or sensitive to the feelings of others.

They can get anxious or depressed over failure to achieve the results they want but get over it quickly. As a child they can be defiant to parental authority or any authority.

A father of a Choleric-Melancholy told me that when his son was six years old they went out to eat at a restaurant. The waiter was slow responding to serve them. His son quickly got on top of the table and screamed at the waiter to come to their table! He did! The father of the Choleric-Melancholy child was Phlegmatic and was slow to respond to the lack of service so his son took over!

The Choleric is more likely to cause others to go to counseling than go themselves.

Phlegmatic

The Phlegmatic blends are the Phlegmatic-Choleric, Phlegmatic-Sanguine, and Phlegmatic-Melancholy. The Phlegmatic temperament is not likely to seek counseling because of their passive nature.

The core drive of the Phlegmatic is to avoid conflict of even the slightest kind. They rarely show emotions and have a stoic expression. They have a very difficult time making a decision out of fear not everyone will be pleased with their choice.

They demonstrate patience which is their way of avoiding conflict. They fear change and cling to an established routine. They are very family oriented. Because of their passive nature they are highly likely to endure an abusive relationship. They are so stubborn that they will resist change even if it is in their best interest.

When they do seek counseling it is usually for anxiety and depression that is related to someone trying to change something in their life or excessive concern over a family member, especially their children.

It is very difficult for the Phlegmatic (regardless of blend) to change their feelings about someone or a situation. Once their feelings toward someone turns negative they will not change.

They show passive-aggressive behavior which is a way of indirectly showing negative feelings instead of openly expressing them.

The Phlegmatic can easily lie about anything, especially the Phlegmatic-Sanguine. The Phlegmatic part wants to avoid conflict and the Sanguine parts wants to be accepted.

Melancholy

The Melancholy blends are Melancholy-Choleric, Melancholy-Sanguine, and the Melancholy-Phlegmatic. The Melancholy will likely seek counseling frequently.

The core drive of the Melancholy is to determine what is right and best. They are *not* driven to *be right*, they are driven to find out *what is right*. Their nature is to over analyze a situation, worry excessively, and anticipate problems.

They have a pessimistic outlook on life. They need lots of alone time and a plan to function without anxiety. Their counseling needs centers around anxiety, depression, being obsessive compulsive, and suicidal thoughts.

The Melancholy, regardless of blend, has a very active thought life. They think too much about, well, everything. They analyze what was said to them and what was not said. The analyze between the lines and question other's motives.

They have difficulty going to sleep because they are analyzing the events of the day or a perceived problem. The are sensitive to how others speak to them and criticism of their work.

When the Melancholy-Phlegmatic has the Choleric as their third temperament they become a perfectionist. Perfectionist have a difficult time living in an imperfect world.

A young mother of two came to see me. As soon as she sat down she said, "I hate myself!" I was surprised to hear that. She was a very beautiful lady. Why would she say such a thing?

Turns out she had the perfectionist pattern (Melcholy-Phlegmatic-Choleric) and she was having trouble living what she thought was an imperfect life. She married a wonderful man, had two terrific children, and lived in a house that was perfectly decorated. I explained to her that she has a voice in her head that says, no matter what she does, you can do it better. I explained that the voice was not her friend. She needed to continually say to herself, "I did my best and that's good enough."

Sanguine

The Sanguine temperament blends are Sanguine-Choleric, Sanguine-Phlegmatic, and Sanguine-Melancholy.

The Sanguines seek counseling more than the other three temperaments combined.

The core drives of the Sanguine is to be accepted socially and avoid rejection. The second temperament has *significant* influence on their need for social acceptance.

The Sanguine-Choleric has a need to enjoy social involvement and to be active all the time. The Sanguine-Choleric can have ADD and ADHD as a child. This happens when the Sanguine-Choleric is very intense, i.e., he or she is VERY Sanguine. This person will display a lot of energy and excitement and will move through their day with hardly a break in their activity. At the end of the day they fall asleep quickly.

This blend can be undisciplined in controlling their thinking, emotions, and behavior. The Sanguine-Choleric blend experiences burnout about every three to five weeks. They use so much energy that they "hit the wall" and need one or two days of inactivity to replenish their energy. Then they are off again for another three to five weeks of heavy activity.

The Sanguine-Phlegmatic's core drive is to build and hold relationships. They may have difficulty letting go of a relationship even if it's toxic.

The Sanguine-Phlegmatic rarely seeks counseling because they tend to be well-balanced emotionally. They are driven to have lots of relationships. Once a relationships is formed (like in kindergarten) they tend to keep the relationship throughout their lifespan. They tend to be tolerant and accepting of others and avoid most of the emotional and mental struggles the other Sanguine blends have.

The Sanguine-Melancholy

The Sanguine-Melancholy is the temperament blend that seeks counseling more than all the other temperament blends combined.

The reason is this blend is composed of two opposite and opposing temperaments. The Sanguine part (extroverted) is the biggest and pulls the person toward social activity. The Melancholy (introverted) pulls the person toward privacy. This creates tension for the individual that is difficult to manage. The core issue due to this combination is a fear of rejection which causes a high level of anxiety and sensitivity.

If this tension is not managed it will cause natural shifts in mood, even mood swings. They can go from being up and happy to being down and feeling depressed in a moment.

The shifts in their moods are typically caused by one of two things (or both). First, the fear of rejection is a core drive that causes them to be sensitive to what people say to them and how others treat them. They have a natural need to look favorable in the eyes of others and when a negative response is perceived, and they feel rejected, a sudden burst of emotion may occur followed by isolation.

Second, the have a need to be alone and when this doesn't happen daily they become irritated and their mood shifts. They then seek the opportunity to be away from others to be alone.

The Sanguine and Melancholy combinations creates a natural push/pull tension because they are polar opposites. No other combination produces as much internal tension as the Sanguine-Melancholy temperament blend.

This combination can also express the most emotion. They they can get more excited than anyone (Sanguine) and get more depressed than anyone (Melancholy).

The Sanguine-Melancholy is the only temperament blend that can be diagnosed as bipolar. I have worked with several thousand bipolar people while working at the mental hospital and in private practice and everyone was a Sanguine-Melancholy. So bipolar is not the result of a chemical imbalance in the brain or there would be a wide range of temperament blends represented in this diagnosis.

89

The Sanguine-Melancholy has mood swings that are a natural part of their temperament blend. When this temperament blend is not managed well they also attract the diagnosis of BPD (Borderline Personality Disorder), DID (Dissociative Identity Disorder previously called Multiple Personality Disorder). This blend is also capable of having a psychotic break with reality.

WAIT!_____ WAIT!_____ WAIT!

Now you may be wondering, "Will every Sanguine-Melancholy develop these disorders?" The answer is ABSOLUTELY NOT!

The Sanguine-Melancholy is the most gifted and creative of all the blends. They write songs and sing the songs, these are the actors and actresses, engineers, writes, poets, and the list goes on!

When the Sanguine-Melancholy fails to control their thoughts, emotions, and behavior they invite a diagnosis.

PART IV

God's Wisdom

Chapter 17

God's Wisdom

God's wisdom as to why we have mental, emotional, and behavioral problems in life isn't complicated. The solution isn't either.

Review Man's wisdom (the medical model) teaches that the environment in which a person is raised, or a person's inherited genes, or the malfunctioning of a person's brain is the cause of problems. Since these things are proven not to be true, we only have the individual's choices left to explain extreme behavior.

This is actually good news because by following man's wisdom you are a victim of your circumstances, your genes, and/or your brain chemistry. This logic teaches that an individual has no power over what has happened in the past or what will happen in the future without the help of medications.

What then does the Bible teach about extreme behavior? The Bible says three things about behavior.

1. All Behavior is a Choice

Nowhere in the Bible does it suggest that behavior is caused by something other than a person making a choice. In Genesis 3:6 the woman and Adam both made the choice to eat of the fruit from the forbidden tree. The evil one was there influencing them but they both made the choice to eat of the fruit.

Throughout the Bible directives are given to stop doing something or start doing something. The Ten Commandments in Exodus 20 are things we are to choose to do and not do. Note Joshua 24:15.

*And if it seems evil to you to serve the Lord, **choose** for yourselves this day whom you will serve, whether the gods which your fathers served that were on the other side of the River, or the gods of the Amorites, in whose land you dwell. But as for me and my house, we will serve the Lord.*

Every book in the New Testament encourages us to choose: *put on, put off,* or *stop* this and *start* that. Ephesians 6:11 is one example.

Put on the whole armor of God, that you may be able to stand against the wiles of the devil.

The Bible is clear, God holds each person accountable. Romans 14:12; *So then each of us shall give account of himself to God.*

There will be no excuses or blame shifting when you stand before God. Everyone will have to give an account of choices made.

Generational curse? There are some who believe that the Bible teaches there is a generational curse. That is, some are prone to some specific sin such as excessive alcohol consumption, anxiety, and depression because they are cursed. If this is true and you are cursed to drink alcohol excessively, or easily become anxious, or depressed, then you are not responsible for your actions because of the curse.

The idea comes from Exodus 20:5-6 where the Ten Commandments are listed in verses 1-14. Here are verses 5-6 from which some believe teach a generational curse:

5 you shall not bow down to them [idols] *nor serve them. For I, the Lord your God, am a jealous God, visiting the iniquity of the fathers upon the children to the third and fourth generations of those who hate Me, 6 but showing mercy to thousands, to those who love Me and keep My commandments.*

The idea of a "generational curse" does not appear in the Bible. The context of verses 5-6 is about having false images in place of God and the **consequence** of doing such a thing. Generations to follow will be influenced by the choice to worship an idol. The consequences are so severe that it will influence as many as four generations that follow!

2. Behavior can be influenced

Behavior can be influenced by Satan, the Holy Spirit, or other people.

Satan The first influence recorded in the Bible is in Genesis 3:1-6 as mentioned. Satan, in the form of a serpent, influenced the woman to doubt what God had said. Based on the words of Satan the woman ate the fruit and gave it to Adam who was standing beside her, made a choice and also ate. The result was that sin entered the human race.

The Holy Spirit John 14:26 identifies what the Spirit of God does for believers.

> *But the Helper, the Holy Spirit, whom the Father will send*
> *in My name, He will teach you all things, and bring to*
> *your remembrance all things that I said to you.*

Other People Throughout the Bible God warns us to choose wisely with whom we spend time because of the possible negative influence others can have. Someone has said that we become like the average of the seven people with whom we spend the most time. Solomon wrote the book of Proverbs to help his son avoid the pitfalls of life and sinful people. Note the following advice:

Proverbs 1:10   *My son, if sinful men entice you,*
                  do not give in to them.

We, of course, have no control over what environment we are born into, nor do we select our parents. The early influence of the people that raised us can have either a positive or negative impact. It's during this time that we develop a sense of self, sense of value, and sense of worthy of being loved.

During our life other people can have an impact on our outlook either directly or indirectly. For example, hearing a speaker, watching a movie, and the friends we make all have the possibility of having a positive or negative impact on our development. We are warned to choose carefully the people with whom we spend time:

Proverbs 13:20

> *He who walks with wise men will be wise,*
> *But the companion of fools will be destroyed.*

1 Corinthians 15:33

> *Do not be deceived: Evil company corrupts*
> *good habits.*

3. Extreme behavior is caused by a lack of self-control

A. Proverbs 22:6

> *Train up a child in the way he should go,*
> *and when he is old he will not depart from it.*

Proverb 22:6 has two possible interpretations. It can either refer to training a child according to *God's* way (i.e., teach wisdom), or it can refer to training a child according to the *child's* way (i.e., teach self-control).

Strong's Hebrew and Greek Dictionary shows the meaning of the word translated *train up* to include the idea *to narrow* (by implication to *throttle*). So when you are *training* a child, you are *narrowing, reducing,* or *throttling* the child's *behavior*, thereby teaching *self-control.*

The Hebrew phrase translated *in the way he should go*, according to *Brown-Driver-Briggs Hebrew* dictionary, is literally *according to the mouth of his way* and can, therefore, be rendered *according to his way.* The point is to train a child according to their individual *way* or characteristics which helps the child develop self-control.

Since this is a proverb, it is mostly true, however, it is not always true. Parents can do all they need to do but it is up to the child to respond favorably to the parents instructions.

My brother, Dr. Mike Cocoris, comments on Proverbs 22:6 in *Proverbs, The Path To Wisdom*, 2014, page 178:

> "The seed sown in childhood is bound to come to harvest in adulthood" (Unger). The Danish proverb says "What youth learns, age does not forget." "The man will be, as the child is trained" (Delitzsch).

This Proverb is teaching that parents need to *narrow* a child's behavior, thereby helping the child learn self-control. Since each child has their own "way" some need more *narrowing* than others. A child's "way" is based on their specific heart attitude and temperament. Learning self-control early in life is critical to success in life.

B. Proverbs 16:32

> *He who is slow to anger is better than the mighty.*
> *And he who rules his spirit than he who takes a city.*

The contrast in this verse is between having great *physical strength* verses having *self-control*.

First, you are far better to be slow to express anger than one who is physically very strong.

Second, if you control your spirit or temper, you are better that one who can capture a city. The idea is that you are so physically strong that you can not only *capture* a city but you alone can *keep* the city under your control!

C. Proverbs 25:28

> *Whoever has no rule over his own spirit is like*
> *a city broken down, without walls.*

The contrast in this verse is between one who cannot control his spirit or temper and a city with no walls. The walls were there but now they are gone! The city is left defenseless! The message is clear, a person is easily defeated without self-control.

D. Proverbs 6:9 You can *sleep* too much.

> *How long will you slumber, O sluggard?*
> *When will you rise from your sleep?*

E. Proverbs 10:19 You can *talk* too much.

> *In the multitude of words sin is not lacking,*
> *But he who restrains his lips is wise.*

Proverbs 17:28

> *Even fools are thought wise if they keep silent,*
> *and discerning if they hold their tongues.*

F. Proverbs 12:25 You can be *too concerned.*

Anxiety in the heart of man causes depression,
But a good word makes it glad.

G. Proverbs 23:20-21 You can *eat* too much.

20 Do not mix with winebibbers, Or with gluttonous
eaters of meat; 21 For the drunkard and the glutton
will come to poverty, And drowsiness will clothe a
man with rags.

H. Proverbs 23:29-35 *You can drink too much.* Notice
the details of the results of drinking too much:

29 Who has woe? Who has sorrow? Who has contentions?
Who has complaints? Who has wounds without cause?
Who has redness of eyes? 30 Those who linger long at
the wine, Those who go in search of mixed wine.

See the rest of Proverb 23:31-35 for more results of
drinking too much.

I. Proverbs 29:11 You can *express too much emotion.*

A fool vents all his feelings. But a wise man holds
them back.

The Hebrew word for *fool* means *stupid.* The Hebrew word
for *wise* means *learned, skillful.* The person who lacks self-control
will express his/her emotions without restraint. A wise person will
not. The verse is clearly teaching that it is possible to control the
display of emotion. If you do, you are wise. If you don't you are
a fool.

Proverbs 20:3

*It is to one's honor to avoid strife, but every fool
is quick to quarrel.*

Senator John Kennedy of Louisiana (2025) said, "Life is hard,
it's harder when you're stupid."

Self-control is the result of a person deciding to control his/her
thoughts, feelings, desires, behavior, and speech. It is the result of
allowing the Spirit of God to do His work in your life.

Conclusion

God's wisdom is clear. We are all responsible for the choices we
make. We are all accountable for what we think, feel, do, and
say.

We can be influenced by Satan, the Holy Spirit, and others
Extreme thinking, feeling, and behavior is caused by a lack of
self-control.

Chapter 18

The Cause is a Lack of Self-Control

If mental, emotional, or behavioral issues are not caused by a lack of *self-control*, how then do they develop? Is it some magical something yet to be discovered or it as simple as these issues are caused by a lack of controlling thoughts, feelings, and behavior?

People who do not have self-control allow extreme expressions of what they think, feel, do, and what they say.

Since the chemical imbalance theory is not true, since there is no proof of generically transmitted mental, emotional, and behavioral issues, since the environment cannot cause behavior (only expose one to influence), there is only one option left:

People disturb themselves by failing to control
their thoughts, feelings, and behavior.

Not only does the Bible point out the importance of self-control, and the consequences when it's absent, but it's importance is recognized outside the Bible.

From the Bible

Let's take a closer look at what the Bible says about self-control. Romans 7:19-20 explains why we struggle with issues such as the ones we are discussing in this book. The apostle Paul makes it clear that we *struggle* because we live in a sinful body.

For the good that I will to do, I do not do; but the evil I will not to do, that I practice. 20 Now if I do what I will not to do, it is no longer I who do it, but sin that dwells in me.

We can all identify with the Apostle Paul. We struggle with unhealthy thoughts and desires that sometimes spill over into unhealthy even destructive behavior. And who hasn't expressed strong feelings that they later regretted? We struggle because we all have a sin nature that we inherited from Adam.

The apostle Paul wrote the epistle to the Romans around 57 AD. However, Paul had already written the epistle of Galatians around 49 AD. So, Paul's understanding of our struggle, in detail, had already been written in Galatians 5:16-26:

16 I say then: Walk in the Spirit, and you shall not fulfill the lust of the flesh. 17 For the flesh lusts against the Spirit, and the Spirit against the flesh; and these are contrary to one another, so that you do not do the things that you wish. 18 But if you are led by the Spirit, you are not under the law. 19 Now the works of the flesh are evident, which are: adultery, fornication, uncleanness, lewdness, 20 idolatry, sorcery, hatred, contentions, jealousies, outbursts of wrath, selfish ambitions, dissensions, heresies, 21 envy, murders, drunkenness, revelries, and the like; of which I tell you beforehand, just as I also told you in time past, that those who practice such things will not inherit the kingdom of God. 22 But the fruit of the Spirit is love, joy, peace, longsuffering, kindness, goodness, faithfulness, 23 gentleness, self-control. Against such there is no law. 24 And those who are Christ's have crucified the flesh with its passions and desires. 25 If we live in the Spirit, let us also walk in the Spirit. 26 Let us not become conceited, provoking one another, envying one another.

It is clear that if you live according to the *flesh* (your standards) you are capable of producing some, if not all, of the behavior that is listed in verses 16-21. It is also clear that if you live according to the *Spirit* you will see some, most, or all of the behavior in your life that is listed in verses 22-26.

Notice, the final characteristic of the fruit of the Spirit is *self-control*. This suggest that God does not intend to overcome our will and turn us into a robot. We are expected to, and responsible for, controlling our own thoughts, feelings, and behavior.

In Galatians 5:23, "self-control" (temperance, NKJV) is the translation of the Greek word *enkrateia*, which means "*possessing power, strong, having mastery or possession of, self-controlled*" (Kenneth S. Wuest, *Word Studies in the Greek New Testament*, "Galatians," p. 160). *Vincent's Word Studies of the New Testament* adds that it means "*holding in hand the passions and desires*" (vol.

IV, p. 168). The word refers, therefore, to the mastery or control over the expression of one's desires and impulses.

Being in control of "self " means that you **withhold** the expression of what you think, what you feel, and what you want to say and do when it is inappropriate or it would cause harm to yourself or to someone else.

As mentioned, Proverbs 16:32 (NLT) states, *Better to be patient than powerful; better to have self-control than to conquer a city.*

Also, as mentioned, Proverbs 25:28 states that *Whoever has no rule over his own spirit is like a city broken down, without walls.* This proverbs shows the *consequences* of a lack of self-control. The imagery is that of a city that does not have walls so they are easily overwhelmed and defeated!

The Bible is clear, controlling your thoughts, feelings, and behavior is necessary to avoid being defeated.

The following are exerts from my brother's book, *The Spiritual Life, Clarifying the Confusion*, 2011, 2014, 2024, Dr. G. Michael Cocoris. To successfully live the spiritual life one must have self-control as Mike discusses:

Peter says to knowledge, add self-control (2 Pet. 1:6). Two New Testament Greek words contain self-control. One, used in Titus 1:8; 2:2, 4, 5, 6, 12, etc., means to be sensible and self-controlled. The other, which appears here, seems to focus more on self-control (Gal. 5:22; the verb form occurs in 1 Cor. 7:9; 9:25). Green says that self-control is controlling your passions instead of being controlled by them.

This Greek word for self-control occurs in Galatians 5:22. The fruit of the Spirit is self-control, which raises the issue of God-control. Many believers today speak of spiritual life as if it is all God-controlled. That flies in the face of Scriptural statements about believers being responsible for controlling themselves.

Breeze argues that the believer is "not a thoughtless, unwilling puppet." He adds, "To say that the Holy Spirit controls us is a less-than-accurate description of the relationship between the believer and his Lord. It is rather true that He instructs us, He leads us, and we, by doing the will of God, perform heaven's purposes. The call is not for the believer to abandon himself to God. Rather he is called to responsible, thoughtful, willful obedience.

Our commitment to Christ should not be presented as self-abandonment but as self-control.

The New Testament itself mentions areas that need self-control. In some of these, the Greek word for self-control is used, but in others, it is not.

<u>Believers are to control their sexual desires</u> (1 Cor. 7:9). According to the Scripture, there are two solutions to sexual sin. The first is to flee. Paul says, "Flee sexual immorality" (1 Cor. 6:18). The second solution is to get married. Paul says, "But I say to the unmarried and to the widows: It is good for them if they remain even as I am; but if they cannot exercise self-control, let them marry. For it is better to marry than to burn with passion" (1 Cor. 7:8-9).

<u>Believers are to control their thoughts</u>. Peter says, "Therefore gird up the loins of your mind, be sober, and rest your hope fully upon the grace that is to be brought to you at the revelation of Jesus Christ" (1 Pet. 1:13). This is a passage where the word "self-control" does not appear,

but the idea is clearly there. The way to control the mind is by thinking about something else. Paul exhorts, "Finally, brethren, whatever things are true, whatever things are noble, whatever things are just, whatever things are pure, whatever things are lovely, whatever things *are* of good report, if *there is* any virtue and if *there is* anything praiseworthy—meditate on these things" (Phil. 4:8).

Believers are to control their emotions. "Let all bitterness, wrath, anger, clamor, and evil speaking be put away from you, with all malice. And be kind to one another, tenderhearted, forgiving one another, just as God in Christ forgave you" (Eph. 4:31-32). Again, the word self-control does not appear, but the concept is present.

Believers are to control their tongues. "For we all stumble in many things. If anyone does not stumble in word, he *is* a perfect man, able also to bridle the whole body" (Jas. 3:2). America is becoming a nation of angry, short-tempered people. From road rage to airplane rage, grocery store rage, and violence at youth sports events, there are emotional outbursts with unprecedented frequency.

Believers are to exercise self-control in every area of life. Paul says, "And everyone who competes *for the prize* is temperate in all things. Now they *do it* to obtain a perishable crown, but we *for* an imperishable *crown*" (1 Cor. 9:25). The word rendered "temperate" is the Greek word "self-control."

God's wisdom is clear, it is necessary to control your thoughts, feelings, and behavior to live a life free of extremes.

When you routinely choose to control your thoughts, feelings, and behavior you develop *habits* of thinking that become *patterns* of behaving which become a healthy and appropriate *lifestyle* way of living.

Outside the Bible

Epictetus (55-135 C. E.)
People are capable of disturbing themselves. This is by no means a new idea; it's been around for thousands of years. Epictetus, a Greek philosopher said:

> *People are disturbed, not by things or events, but by the views (perceptions) which they take of them.*

It's not what happens to you that causes you to be upset, it's what you *think about* what happens to you that causes you to be upset. It's not the event, it's your interpretation of the event. Let's illustrate:

Imagine that we are walking down the sidewalk toward a restaurant for lunch. Suddenly we notice a car pull over across the street. The man jumps out of the car yelling at his rear tire that went flat. He kicks the tire! He throws his coat in the back seat, flings open the trunk, gets the car jack out, throws it on the ground and begins changing the tire. What could he be thinking? He's clearly upset so he may be thinking, "Why me, why now, why this?" "I'm going to get dirty and I'll be late for my appointment!"

109

We look up and another car with a flat tire pulled over on our side of the street! Wow, what are the chances? He has our attention as he gets out of the car. He looks at the flat tire, takes his coat off and puts it in the back seat. He finds the car jack lays it on the ground and quietly begins to change the tire. What could he be thinking? Well we notice that he is not upset, he's just changing the tire. So, he could be thinking, "These things happen, I'll be late for my appointment but I'll call ahead to let them know. I'll clean up when I get there."

Now both men had a flat tire. Was it the tire going flat that upset the first guy? No. It's what he thought about the tire going flat. It's interfering with my schedule, I'll get dirty, it's inconvenient, etc. The second man also had a flat tire but he did not get upset. Why? He looked at it differently than the first guy. Flat tires happen and he adjusted to the unexpected event.

What can we learn from this illustration? Two guys had a flat tire and there were two different responses to the same kind of event. The first man immediately *choose* negative thoughts and feelings about his tire going flat. He then chose to act out his feelings with aggression toward the flat tire. His thoughts were negative, his feelings were negative, and his behavior demonstrated anger.

The second man also had a flat but *choose* to respond differently. Instead of having negative thoughts he choose to look at it as *things like this happen in life*. He may have thought that "If I get angry it would not change the fact that my tire is flat." Because his thoughts were positive his feelings followed and he was not upset.

The first man disturbed himself by the choices he made, he did not exercise self-control. The second man did exercise self-control and chose not to get upset about the tire going flat.

The lesson is clear, the one who did not get upset was the one who had *self-control* and chose to look at the flat tire as it was not an upsetting event.

It's not WHAT happens to you that causes you to be upset, it's what you THINK about what happens. How different would your life be if you did not get upset over things like a flat tire?

William Glasser, MD (1925-2013)
William Glasser (psychiatrist) was a strong voice against biological psychiatry. He was against the purpose and use of medications to treat mental, emotional, and behavioral issues as previously discussed. The following excerpts are from his book *Choice Theory, A New Psychology of Personal Freedom*, 1999, pages 1-24.

Suppose you could ask all the people in the world who are not hungry, sick, or poor, people who seem to have a lot to live for, to give you an honest answer to the question, 'How are you?' Millions would say, 'I'm miserable.' If asked why, almost all of them would blame someone else for their misery—lovers, wives, husbands, exes, children, parents, teachers, students, or people they work with. There is hardly a person alive who hasn't been heard saying, 'You're driving me crazy. . . . That really upsets me. . . . Don't you have any consideration for how I feel? . . . You make me so mad, I can't see straight.' It never crosses their minds that they are choosing the misery they are complaining about.

Choice theory explains that, for all practical purposes, we choose everything we do, including the misery we feel. Other people can neither make us miserable nor make us happy. All we can get from them or give to them is *information*. But by itself, *information* cannot make us do or feel anything. It goes into our brains where we process it and then decide what to do. As I explain in great detail in this book, we choose all our actions and thoughts and, indirectly, almost all our feelings and much of our physiology ... Choice theory teaches we are much more in control of our lives than we realize [or willing to admit].

Epictetus and Dr. Glasser are separated by two thousand years yet they both realized the same truth. People are capable of causing their own misery by the way they perceive and interpret the events in their life.

I know that some will say, "But you don't know my circumstances!" I agree and understand that some circumstances are beyond comprehension and extremely difficult.

Viktor E. Frankl , MD (1905 –1997)

Perhaps the most powerful illustration I can offer that individuals are in control of their behavior and responsible for their choices, regardless of their environment or circumstances, comes from Victor Frankl. He was an Austrian psychiatrist and holocaust survivor, who founded logotherapy, a school of psychotherapy.

He and his family were imprisoned in a German concentration camp during WWII. Dr. Frankl's 1946 book *Man's Search for Meaning* chronicles his experience as a prisoner and describes his method of finding a reason to live. Dr. Frankl explained in one statement how he survived the unthinkable that he endured. He watched every member of his family die except his sister yet he made this statement: ***Everything can be taken from a man or a woman but one thing: the last of human freedoms to choose one's attitude in any given set of circumstances, to choose one's own way.***

What do psychologists say about self-control?

The following are exerts from an article written by Cherry Kendra and can be found at https://www.verywellmind.com/kendra-cherry-2794702 (emphasis added).

Psychologists typically define self-control as: The ability to control behaviors to avoid temptations and achieve goals. The ability to delay gratification and resist unwanted behaviors or urges. A limited resource that can be depleted. People use various terms for self-control, including discipline, determination, grit, willpower, and fortitude...but it is also a skill you can strengthen with practice.

Self-control is one aspect of executive function, a set of abilities that helps people to plan, monitor, and achieve their goals. People with attention-deficit attention disorder (ADHD) often have characteristics linked to problems with executive function. There are three primary types of self-control:

Impulse control refers to the ability to manage urges and impulses. People who struggle with impulse control act first without thinking about the consequences of their actions.

Emotional control refers to the ability to regulate emotional responses. Someone who struggles with emotional control may find it hard to manage strong emotions. They may overreact, experience lasting bad moods, and get overwhelmed by the intensity of their feelings.

Movement control refers to the ability to control how and when the body moves. A person who has difficulty with movement control may experience restlessness and find it difficult to remain still. A self-controlled person exhibits a great deal of willpower and personal control. They don't act impulsively and can regulate their emotions and actions effectively.

How important is self-control in your day-to-day life?
A Stress in America survey conducted by the American Psychological Association (APA) found that 27% of respondents identified a lack of willpower as the primary factor keeping them from reaching their goals. The majority of people surveyed (71%) believed that self-control can be both learned and strengthened. Researchers have found that people who have better self-control tend to be **healthier and happier**, both in the short term and in the long term.

   In one influential experiment, students who exhibited greater self-discipline had better grades, higher test scores, and were more likely to be admitted to a competitive academic program. The study also found that when it came to academic success, self-control was a more important factor than IQ scores.

Summary. Missing from our thinking is often the basic truth that we disturb ourselves because of the choices we make.

Many look for ways to blame others and circumstances for their thinking, feelings, and behavior without considering that the problem is coming from within. A mirror reveals the true source of our misery.

When anyone disturbs themselves frequently to the point where it interferes with their lifestyle and they take medication to relieve the symptoms then change in the way they think is needed.

The evidence is abundant in the Bible and outside the Bible that a lack of self-control can lead to a *lifestyle* that is unhealthy, inappropriate, or even destructive

The question now becomes, "How do I gain control over what I think, feel, do, and say?"

Chapter 19

How To Overcome Mental, Emotional, & Behavioral Issues

To you who may be struggling, it is good news to know that the mental, emotional, or behavioral issues you are having is the result of a lack of self-control. Why? Because you are not the victim of faulty brain chemistry, genetics, or a bad environment. You are where you are because of the choices you have made.

The choices you made turned around and made you.

You can reverse where you are by making different choices that will lead to the control of what you think, feel, and do.

Of course, you may need guidance and support from others along your journey but you are capable of reversing the issues you are having. It starts with accepting responsibility for your past choices followed by a decision to change the way you have been thinking. Here are the steps to a better way of living:

1. Accept *responsibility* for the choices you have made.
2. Decide to change.
3. Ask God to help you change.
4. Change what you have been thinking.

STEP 1
Accept Responsibility For Your Choices

Before you can move forward to a better way of living you must accept responsibility for the choices that you have made. From those choices you developed patterns of thinking, feeling, and behaving that are causing the issue/s with which you are now struggling. Do not blame-shift.

STEP 2
Decide To Change

Change starts with a decision. You must *decide* that you want too reverse and overcome the unhealthy patterns of thinking, feeling, and behaving that you have developed.

This sounds simple, or even easy, but it's actually the hardest part! Everyone that has changed their behavior first accepted responsibility for their choices and made the decision to change. It does not matter what kind of therapist you've seen or how many times, *change* occurs when *you* make the *decision* to change.

One older gentleman told me that he had a certain issue and that a therapist told him there was no cure. I said to him "That is not true. If that were true it means that you have ceased being human and you are no longer able to make a decision." I told him, "By believing that there is no cure, you have given yourself permission to continue the activity." This man did not want to change and he had been given an excuse to continue the activity.

118

Those who change want to,
those who do not change do not want to.

Here are a few examples of decisions that people have made:

I decided I wanted the award. Aaron Meyers was a friend of mine who was a very successful salesperson. He was asked to speak to the company's sales force of 600 people to help them become more successful. Here is what he said:

> I have received lots of awards selling. If you want to be on stage to receive an award you have to *first decide you want to be up here.* I have noticed that those who were receiving an award said in their acceptance speech, "I was sitting in the audience last year and *"I decided that I wanted that award next year."* If you want to be up here next year, *decided right now* that you will do everything necessary to get an award."

I've been a corporate consultant for many years and observed that there is a correlation between successful salespeople and mentally strong people. Aaron's advice to the group was to set a goal and decide to work toward achieving it. This is what I'm saying. If you want to get over where you are mentally, emotionally, or behaviorally, then **decide** to change and then work on it.

Some of those who heard Aaron speak **decided** they wanted an award and set a goal to achieve it. They changed some habits, worked hard, overcame obstacles, and achieved the award the next year.

It never occurred to her. When I worked at the mental hospital a young lady came in with her mother for help with an addiction to cocaine. She had great difficulty answering one question:

> During the interview I asked her, "Why do you use cocaine?" She paused for a moment and said, "I'm a college student and the pressure is overwhelming." I said, "Wrong answer, why do you use cocaine?" She thought for a moment and said, "Oh, it's my dad because he's on me all the time!" I said, "Wrong answer, why do you use cocaine?" She became a little frustrated and after a moment she said, "It's my boyfriend, we are not getting along right now." I again said, "Wrong answer, why do you use cocaine?" She was now getting a bit agitated and said it was her mother (who was sitting beside her). And again I said, "Wrong answer, why do you use cocaine?"
>
> She had exhausted all of the excuses she could think of and now very frustrated she said, "Okay, you tell me, why do I use cocaine?" I said to her, "Because you choose to." She relaxed and sat back in her chair and said, "I never thought about that!" I said to her why don't you go home and think about that and come back."
>
> Two weeks later she came back and asked to speak to me. She said, "I thought about what you said and *I decided* that if I chose to do cocaine I could choose not to use cocaine!" She was now on her way to recovery because she accepted responsibility and made the decision to stop.

Some believe that they cannot control their thoughts, feelings, or behavior. If you believe you can't, you can't. If you believe you can, you can. Change is one decision away from beginning the journey to a new way of living.

She said no. I had one client that I worked with off/on for four years. She was married with three children and now in her early fifties. Her issue was anger. Here is her story:

She was angry about everything in her life. Most of her anger was directed toward her husband. She thought nothing was going right in her life. He had moved her to Texas from another state and she hated her husband for it, she hated her very expensive home, and she hated the state of Texas. I tried everything I knew to do and nothing worked. Finally, she came to me and said she had ruined her marriage with her mouth. She ask me to help her deal with her anger issues. I said I will walk down the path with you and we will work though it together. She came back the next week and the next. On the third visit back she said this, "I cannot do this, I feel naked without my anger!"

She said she could not bring herself to stop being angry at anything and everything. At least she was honest. I told her since that is your decision you can expect things to get worse in your life. They did and she got the divorce she wanted from her husband. By the way, her husband was one of the finest people I have ever known.

He said okay. One older gentleman, who had been an alcoholic most of his life, told me this story:

His routine was to buy two bottles of Vodka at a time and put them both in separate brown bags and put them both under the drivers seat. On the way to work and back home he would sip on one of the bottles until it was empty and start on the remaining bottle. After he emptied the second bottle he returned to the liquor store and would buy two more. He did this for 10 years until one day as he pulled into his driveway his son came out to meet him. Something was different, his son had never met him that way. He quickly rolled down the window to greet his son. His son said, "Dad, you have a grandson that you have never taken the time to get to know. Would you please stop drinking and get to know you grandson?" The man said to me that he look at his son and looked at the bottle and decided to stop, and said "Okay."

He then poured out the remaining Vodka immediately and never touched it again. He then told me the second bottle of vodka stayed under his seat so long that the brown paper sack fell apart.

The grandfather was met with a decision to stop drinking so he could get to know his grandson. He decided at that moment that he had a purpose to stop drinking. He followed through with his decision when all he had to do was reach under his seat. Temptation was inches away but it didn't matter, he had decided!

He thought he had decided. A young man in his late twenties came to see me because he had a problem viewing pornography. Here's his story:

He was caught viewing pornography three years earlier by his wife and was just caught again. He said that he had decided back then to stop. I said to him, "No you didn't." He disagreed and said, "Yes I did." I said, "You didn't shut the door, you left it slightly open thinking that one day you would do it again." He paused, looked away and then said,

"You're right, I left the door open."

I explained to him that he never decided to stop or he would have stopped. So, I asked him, "Are you now ready to make the decision to stop?" He thought about it for a moment and then said, "Yes!" I looked at my watch and said, "Okay, it is now 2:00, remind yourself, I've made the decision to stop at 2:00 on this date." I then told him to write down the date and if tempted remember that this was the date you decided to stop.

You will know if you made the decision by whether or not you're able to follow through with the decision. If you don't follow through with your decision then you never really decided.

To follow through means you may struggle but you do not give in!

A remarkable reversal. When I worked at the mental hospital I was on a team of therapists that responded to Dallas, Texas area hospitals that had someone come to the emergency room with a mental health crisis. My job was to evaluate the person to determine if they needed in hospital treatment. Here is the story of one of those visits. This one happened at 2:00 A.M.

Upon arrival, the ER doctor explained a young man was there because his wife had left him and was living in a crack house addicted to cocaine. He had tried everything to get her back but he had failed. He stopped eating and was severely depressed. He was actually starving himself to death over his grief and love for his wife. Out of desperation his sister brought him to the hospital emergency room. Here's what happened.

His sister told me that her brother and his wife were both Christians. He was sitting in the corner of the room with a blanket over his head. At first he would not talk to me or even look at me, he just sat there with his head down under the blanket.

I asked his sister if I could talk to him about the Bible (she was holding one under her arm). She said yes. I explained to him that God cared more about his wife than he did and that this was God's problem to solve, not his. He had exhausted all of his efforts and now it was time to let God take over. I encouraged him to let God take care of his wayward wife and for him to trust God in what seemed to be an impossible situation. He did not respond.

I turned my attention back to his sister again and after a few minutes had passed I looked over and he had stood up. His attitude was remarkably different. He said, "This is not my problem, it is God's problem!" Turning his attention now to his sister he then said, "I'm hungry, can we get something to eat!" This young man made a remarkable reversal of his emotional state when he made the decision to let God solve his problem.

I had never seen such a remarkable reversal of depressed feelings as I just witnessed nor have I've seen it sense.

STEP 3
Ask God to Help You

To change or reverse what you were thinking when you developed a lifestyle way of thinking that was unhealthy or inappropriate, granted, is difficult. But, as a Christian, you are not expected to fight the battle by yourself. God wants you to trust Him and call on Him for help. Here are two passages to depend on for God's help on your new journey:

A. Proverbs 3:5-7 Trust God.

5 Trust in the Lord with all your heart, And lean not on your own understanding; 6 In all your ways acknowledge Him, And He shall direct your paths. 7 Do not be wise in your own eyes; Fear the Lord and depart from evil.

This passage is teaching that we are to depend on the Lord for guidance and not to trust our own judgement. God knows best so let Him clear the obstacles before you. Don't think you are wise enough to do that yourself. Live God's way which is the core thought in this book.

B. Hebrews 4:16 Ask God to help you.

Let us, therefore, come boldly to the throne of grace, that we may obtain mercy and find grace to help in time of need.

This passage is teaching that God wants you to ask Him for help when you need mercy and grace.

I have written a book about how to Biblically handle trials, *Trust God No Matter What!*, John T. Cocoris, 2026. My brother, Dr. G. Michael Cocoris, has written a must read book on living the spiritual life; *The Spiritual Life, Clarifying The Confusion*, 2011, 2024. Both books are available on Amazon and Barnes and Nobles.

STEP 4
Change What You Have Been Thinking

If you are struggling with one or more mental, emotional, or behavioral issues it is because of past decisions that formed a way of thinking that became a habit. For example, you get anxious because you believe it's okay to get anxious, it's a habit.

To develop a new way of thinking and expressing your emotions and behaving will take time. It will not happen quickly so do not be hard on yourself as you begin your new journey.

Before we get into how and what to change, I want to share an experience a sales manger, Albert Gray, had many decades ago that offers some insight into what is necessary to change.

Albert E. N. Gray (1845-1942)
Albert Gray was an official of the Prudential Insurance Company of America. In 1940 he delivered a message from a booklet he wrote called *The Common Denominator of Success* to the National Association of Life Underwriters at their annual convention.

Albert Gray had figured it out. People who are successful have a reason to succeed and then decided to do those things that people who are not successful do not want to do. Here are some quotes from his booklet:

> The secret of success of every man who has ever been successful lies in the fact that he formed the habit of doing things that non-successful people don't like to do.

Why are successful people able to do things they don't like to do while failures are not? Because successful people have a purpose strong enough to make them form the habit of doing things they don't like to do in order to accomplish the purpose they want to accomplish.

By doing the things they don't like to do, they can accomplish the things they want to accomplish. Successful people are influenced by the desire for pleasing results. Failures are influenced by the desire for pleasing methods and are inclined to be satisfied with such results as can be obtained by doing things they like to do.

Truth is where you find it. Whether you are struggling with mental or emotional issues or trying to be successful in life the requirements are the same.

You have to establish healthy patterns of thinking, feeling, and behaving. You need a purpose that's bigger than yourself to keep you from stumbling along the way. You need to be willing to make choices to do those things that people do to overcome any obstacle.

What do people do that live over the circumstances of life? They have self-control. They accept responsibility for the choices they have made, and at some point in their life, decided to change.

To overcome where you are in life requires doing the things that other people do not want to do; change how you think.

James Allen (1864-1912)
He wrote *As A Man Thinketh* and identified the importance of what a person thinks.

As a man thinketh in his heart so is he, not only embraces the whole of a man's being, but is so comprehensive as to reach out to every condition and circumstance of his life. A man is literally what he thinks, his character being the complete sum of all his thoughts. As the plant springs from, and could not be without, the seed, so every act of a man springs from the hidden seeds of thought, and could not have appeared without them. This applies equally to those acts called "spontaneous" and "unpremeditated" as to those which are deliberately executed.

Romans 12:1-2

This passage teaches that in order for change to occur you have to change what you have been thinking. You need to re-program.

12 I beseech you therefore, brethren, by the mercies of God, that you present your bodies a living sacrifice, holy, acceptable to God, which is your reasonable service. 2 And do not be conformed to this world, but be transformed by the renewing of your mind, that you may prove what is that good and acceptable and perfect will of God.

Romans chapter 12:1 marks a turning point in the epistle. Paul uses the term *therefore* which means he has previously made a point and is now going to apply what he said.

*I beseech you **therefore**, brethren, by the mercies of God, that you present your bodies a living sacrifice, holy, acceptable to God, which is your reasonable service.*

Paul has said that because we have been *justified by faith, we have peace with God* (Romans 5:1). ***Therefore*** Paul strongly encourages (beseech is not a command) us to give ourselves as a *living sacrifice* to Him. It's only *reasonable*, the Greek word means *logical.* So, it's *logical* for us to give back to Him *ourselves* as a *living sacrifice*. How then do we do that?

do not be conformed to his world

First, in verse 2, Paul instructs us to *not be conformed to this world.* The word *conformed* means simply *to be like*. There are two words in the New Testament translated *world*. One is *cosmos* which means *universe*. The other word is *aion* which means age. The word used in verse 2 is *aion*. So Paul is saying that we are not *to be like* the *age* in which we live.

The argument of this book is that we are not to *accept* this *age* of man's wisdom when it comes to the cause of the struggles discussed. Instead, trust God's wisdom to understand the cause and remedy for the issues you may be having.

but be transformed

Next, Christians are to be *transformed by the renewing of our minds*. Transformation is the process we are to go through in order to change. The word *transformation* appears only twice in the New Testament; here in Romans 12:2 and 2 Corinthians 3:18.

You will recognize the Greek word translated "transform" is *metamorphoo* from which we get the word *metamorphosis*. According to *Strong's Hebrew and Greek Dictionary*, this Greek word means *to change to a different pattern, to change into a wholly different form or appearance.*

God has given us an example of *transformation* in nature. Every butterfly begins life as a caterpillar, goes through a *transformation,* and becomes a completely different life form. This is what every believer is to experience in their spiritual life.

I need to get technical to communicate an important truth. The Greek word for transformation (*metamorphoo*) is a verb that is in the present, passive, imperative form. All that means this:

The *present* tense indicates something that is in the process of happening (being transformed). The *passive* voice indicates that the action is produced by a Source outside of the recipient, in this case, "God." The *imperative* mood is a command to keep receiving the transformation.

So, *transformation* (change) happens to you. You *do not* do the changing, you *receive* the change. You are continually responsible to *do* something (mentioned next) and then change will occur. What are you supposed to do continually?

by the renewing of your mind

Now, the meaning of the word *renew* holds the secret as to what anyone must do to change. The word *renew* means to *renovate.*

What happens when you renovate something? You take out the *old* and put in the *new*!

Remodeling a house illustrates renovation. A designer and contractor will take a used, often old home, and make it look brand new. To achieve the makeover they will take out the old fixtures, and sometimes walls, and replace the old fixtures with new ones. When finished it's impossible to see the condition it was once in.

The same process is necessary for someone to change. A person must change (renovate) what they have been thinking that developed issues like anxiety, anger, depression, etc.

Renewing of your mind According to *Thayer's Greek-English Lexicon of The New Testament*, the meaning of the Greek word for *mind* (nous) includes thoughts, feelings, purposes, and desires. So what needs to change is the way you are dealing with life situations. Instead of doing it your way, do it God's way.

Being in control of "self " means that you **withhold** the expression of what you think, what you feel, what you say, and what you want to do and replace it with what God said to do.

For example, there are clear directives in the Bible that instruct us to not be anxious, get angry, or argue with anyone. When you want to do these things, stop! Exercise self-control, don't do it! If you stop (withhold) what you wanted to do you will eventually be transformed according to Romans 12:2. When you are transformed in a particular area like getting angry, you will no longer want to get angry. How great is that! So, being *transformed* means you are becoming more and more like Jesus Christ.

This re-programming of the mind does not take place overnight. It's a lifelong process by which your way of thinking changes to reflect the way God wants you to respond to others and life events.

What's next? Every book in the New Testament has a form of stop/start, put on put off. The next chapters address what is necessary to stop doing and start doing.

Chapter 24

What To *Stop* Doing

To gain *control* over what you think, feel, say, and do you need to *renovate* (change) the way you think. This will take time, lots of time. It's not going to be easy or quick. If you begin doing what God has said you will slowly change into a different person who is in control of "self." Here are five behaviors you need to stop doing to begin your new journey.

1. Stop Getting Anxious

Philippians 4:6-7 *Be anxious for nothing, but in everything by prayer and supplication, with thanksgiving, let your requests be made known to God; 7 and the peace of God, which surpasses all understanding, will guard your hearts and minds through Christ Jesus.*

Anxiety is perhaps the single most damaging habit a Christian can have. To be anxious means that you are worried that the outcome of something important to you will not turn out favorably.

Anxiety is like a door, when left open, lots of others things come in like frustration, anger, and depression.

Proverbs 12:25: *Anxiety in the heart of man causes depression, But a good word makes it glad.*

Anxiety, on some level, plays a part in the issues discussed in this book. The reason anxiety is so destructive is that an anxious person leaves God out of their concern and the solution. Let's look more carefully at Philippians 4:6-7:

> ***Be anxious for nothing***, means we are not permitted to worry about anything. This is a command, not a suggestion.
> ***but in every situation***, means there are no exceptions, ever.
> ***by prayer and petition***, be specific, state your exact concern.
> ***with thanksgiving***, now, thank God for what He is going to do. Be willing to accept the results as God's will.
> ***present your requests to God***, be clear, present the requests to God.
> ***and the peace of God***, means you will have *calm assurance* that God is in control.
> ***which transcends all understanding***, means you will no longer be *troubled* or *anxious*.
> ***will guard your hearts and your minds***, means your thoughts and feelings will be guarded. *Guard* is the greek word *garrison*. This is a military term for guarding something.

If you *choose* not be anxious and you are willing to accept what God will do about your *concern* He will then *guard* your heart. Guard your heart from what? Worry. The word *heart* here includes mind and emotions.

When you accept whatever God chooses to do about your concern is okay with you then peace follows. You will have such peace that you will not be able to understand it or explain it to others.

Anxiety Worksheet

1. What am I **anxious** about? Write it below and be specific?

   _____

2. What is the worst that could happen if my **anxiety** is realized?

   _____

3. What is the probability of me coping if the worst happened?

   ☐ Possible   ☐ Impossible

4. What are three Bible verses that tell me what to do with my **anxiety**?

   ☐ _____
   ☐ _____
   ☐ _____

5. Is my **anxiety** exaggerated?

   ☐ Yes   ☐ No

6. Have I underestimated God's ability to give me peace?

   ☐ Yes   ☐ No

7. An effective way to deal with my **anxiety** is to:

   ☐ Be fearful and worry.
   ☐ Be anxious for nothing! (Philippians 3:5)
   ☐ Trust God and thank Him for whatever He does.

My Plan To Stop Getting Anxious

1. Goal: My goal is to trust God for the outcome of everything that concerns me. I will not be anxious.

2. Reminder. We need to be told once but reminded often. Write this verse on a 3x5 card and keep it with you:

> **Philippians 4:6-7** *Be anxious for nothing, but in everything by prayer and supplication, with thanksgiving, let your requests be made known to God; 7 and the peace of God, which surpasses all understanding, will guard your hearts and minds through Christ Jesus.*

3. Action. When you *realize* that you are getting anxious—**STOP** and **REPLACE** your thoughts by reciting the verse.

When you **STOP** and **REPLACE** your negative thoughts with the verse you are establishing a new way of thinking (making a new habit) and you are one step closer to being transformed as stated in Romans 12:2. Keep working on it and do not be discouraged. It takes time. Ask God to help you.

> **Romans 8:26** *Likewise the Spirit also helps in our weaknesses. For we do not know what we should pray for as we ought, but the Spirit Himself makes intercession for us with groanings which cannot be uttered.*

Do your best to not get anxious and be willing to accept whatever outcome God chooses. You will know you are transformed when you no longer get anxious.

2. Stop Getting Angry

Ephesians 4:26 *Be ye angry and sin not, let not the sun go down on your wrath.*

Righteous indignation is a form of anger that is not considered sin. It is an emotional response over a sense of injustice like the mistreatment of another person. Jesus, for example, drove the money changers out of the temple; Matthew 21: 12-13.

To be an angry person typically means that you experience or express anger frequently, intensely, or in ways that are disruptive to yourself or others.

Being an "angry person" suggests a habit, pattern, or tendency to easily get angry whether you show it outwardly or not.

Characteristics of an Angry Person

Easily irritated: Reacts with anger to minor frustrations or treat others with disdain or indifference.

Frequent outbursts: Regularly loses their temper, sometimes yelling, slamming things, or becoming verbally aggressive or abusive.

Grudge-holding: Holds onto resentment or past wrongs instead of letting things go.

Blames others often: Struggles to take responsibility and tends to externalize blame.

Low patience or tolerance: Easily overwhelmed by stress, leading to frustration or angry outburst.

Difficulty with empathy: May struggle to see others' perspectives during conflicts.

Signs of Chronic Anger

Emotional signs:

- You often feel on edge or irritated.
- You do not let go of insults, betrayals, or disappointments.
- You feel justified, even if others say you're overreacting.
- You get angry quickly.

Physical signs:

- You notice clenched fists, tight jaw, or a racing heart often.
- You feel exhausted or drained after angry episodes.
- You may get headaches, stomachaches, or insomnia connected to stress and anger.

Behavioral signs:

- You raise your voice, argue, slam doors, or break things.
- People say they're afraid to upset you.
- You may express anger through sarcasm, passive-aggressive remarks, or silence.
- You react to others with a bite in your voice.
- You react to others quickly with slight irritation.

Regardless of why you get angry, God says deal with it before sundown. Consider the following passages:

Proverbs 15:1 *A gentle answer turns away wrath, but a harsh word stirs up anger.*

Proverbs 15:18 *A hot-tempered person stirs up conflict, but the one who is patient calms a quarrel.*

Proverbs 19:19 *A man of great wrath will suffer punishment; For if you rescue him, you will have to do it again.*

Ecclesiastes 7:9 *Do not be quickly provoked in your spirit, for anger resides in the lap of fools..*

I Corinthians 13:5 *Love is not provoked.*

Believers are not allowed to get angry but if you do, God says, deal with it quickly; before the sun goes down.

The Fence

There once was a young boy with a very bad temper. The boy's father wanted to teach him a lesson so he gave him a bag of nails and told him that every time he lost his temper he must hammer a nail into their wooden fence.

On the first day of this lesson the little boy had driven 37 nails into the fence. He was really mad! Over the course of the next few weeks the little boy began to control his temper so the number of nails that were hammered into the fence dramatically decreased.

It wasn't long before the little boy discovered it was easier to hold his temper than to drive those nails into the fence. Then, the day finally came when the little boy didn't lose his temper even once and he became so proud of himself he couldn't wait to tell his father.

Pleased, his father suggested that he now pull out one nail for each day that he could hold his temper.

Several weeks went by and the day finally came when the young boy was able to tell his father that all the nails were gone. Very gently the father took his son by the hand and led him to the fence. "You have done very well my son," he smiled and said, "But look at the holes in the fence. The fence will never be the same." The little boy listened carefully as his father continued to speak.

"When you say things in anger they leave permanent scars just like these. And no matter how many times you say you're sorry the wounds will still be there."

My Plan To Stop
Getting Angry

1. Goal: My goal is to stop getting angry.

2. Reminder. We need to be told once but reminded often. Write this verse on a 3x5 card and keep it with you:

> **Ephesians 4:26** *Be ye angry and sin not, let not the sun go down on your wrath.*

3. Action. When you realize that you are getting angry—**STOP** and **REPLACE** your thoughts by reciting the verse.

When you **STOP** and **REPLACE** your negative thoughts with the verse you are establishing a new way of thinking (making a new habit) and you are one step closer to being transformed as stated in Romans 12:2. Keep working on it and do not be discouraged. It takes time. Ask God to help you.

> **Romans 8:26** *Likewise the Spirit also helps in our weaknesses. For we do not know what we should pray for as we ought, but the Spirit Himself makes intercession for us with groanings which cannot be uttered.*

Do your best to not get angry. Ask God to help you. You will know you are transformed when you no longer get angry.

3. Stop Getting Depressed

Proverbs 12:25 *Anxiety in the heart of man causes depression, But a good word makes it glad.*

Normal depression? Some down feelings are normal and appropriate. For example, if you were to lose a loved one to death you would be expected to feel deeply sad emotions and have normal activities like eating, sleeping, and working interrupted. After some time has elapsed these functions return to normal and we continue our journey through this life.

Postpartum depression is often experienced by a mother after childbirth. This is considered a normal response due to hormonal changes, psychological adjustment to motherhood, and fatigue.

Frequent depression is not a chemical imbalance in your brain. There is no scientific evidence that a chemical imbalance in the brain exists that causes depression. It's only a theory. The cause of frequent depression is ...

you are *thinking too much about the wrong thing.*

Those who report they are "depressed" are focused on one or more problems. Life has overwhelmed them, something did not happened as expected, someone did something to them, or they did something to someone else, the list is endless. Some Christians respond to their unwanted circumstances by becoming depressed.

Depression is a feeling of sadness and dejection that alters a person's emotional and mental state and interferes with their daily life functions in varying degrees. Symptoms range from mild to severe and can be short-term or last for an extended period of time.

It is different however when a Christian *routinely* gets depressed over the painful events in their life. It is different when the Christian retreats and withdraws from life to pout or fume about their circumstances. It is different when a Christian reacts negatively to events, gets angry, and depressed.

When depression is a routine response to life's circumstances people are living examples of what Epictetus said 2,000 years ago (as mentioned earlier). Epictetus said that it is not *what* happened to you that is disturbing, it is what you *think about* what happened that is disturbing you.

Depressed people disturb themselves by holding on to their negative perception of the event. If you are depressed you are not trying to solve the problem, you are embedded in the problem by reviewing the negatives and fuming over the wrongness of the event. If you are routinely depressed you are choosing to be miserable.

If you often react this way it is because you fail to see that God is working through your circumstances to conform you into the image of His Son (Romans 8:28-29). Instead of seeing God in the situation you are viewing your circumstance as not fair, wrong, or even punishment from God. The unfairness or wrongness is what is being reviewed and rehearsed in your thoughts. All you can see is the pain and suffering you are going through and you want it to stop ... now! You are stuck in, and focused on, the problem. You fail to see, or do not accept, what God is doing in your life through your circumstances.

Depression and Scripture

The Bible was written over a sixteen-hundred-year period and from the beginning God had something to say about being depressed.

Deuteronomy 31:8 *It is the LORD who goes before you. He will be with you; he will not leave you or forsake you. Do not fear or be dismayed.*

The Hebrew word translated *leave* has the idea of *leave alone.* The word that immediately follows is *forsake* which means to *leave destitute or fail.* The Hebrew word translated *dismayed* means to *break down, either (literally) by violence, or (figuratively) by confusion and fear; to beat down, caused to be discouraged.*

So Moses, the writer of Deuteronomy, has given us three reasons to not be discouraged or depressed. First, God goes before you which means He holds the future and He is leading you. Second, He is with you which means He is beside you. Thirdly, He will never fail you or leave you destitute.

With promises like this, there is no reason to ever be discouraged or depressed. God is there for you and always will be. God continued to encourage us throughout the Bible to wait on Him, to hope in Him, and to humble ourselves before Him as noted in the following verses:

144

Psalms 40:1-3 *I waited patiently for the LORD; he inclined to me and heard my cry. He drew me up from the pit of destruction, out of the miry bog, and set my feet upon a rock, making my steps secure. He put a new song in my mouth, a song of praise to our God. Many will see and fear, and put their trust in the LORD.*

1 Peter 5:6-7 *Humble yourselves therefore under the mighty hand of God, that he may exalt you in due time: Casting all your care upon him; for he careth for you.*

My Plan To Stop Getting Depressed

1. Goal: My goal is to stop getting depressed.

2. Reminder. We need to be told once but reminded often. Write this verse on a 3x5 card and keep it with you:

> **Proverbs 12:25** *Anxiety in the heart of man causes depression, But a good word makes it glad.*

3. Action. When you *realize* that you are getting depressed—**STOP** and **REPLACE** your thoughts by reciting the verse.

When you **STOP** and **REPLACE** your negative thoughts with the verse you are establishing a new way of thinking (making a new habit) and you are one step closer to being transformed as stated in Romans 12:2. Keep working on it and do not be discouraged. It takes time. Ask God to help you.

> **Romans 8:26** *Likewise the Spirit also helps in our weaknesses. For we do not know what we should pray for as we ought, but the Spirit Himself makes intercession for us with groanings which cannot be uttered.*

Do your best to not get depressed. Trust God. You will know you are transformed when you no longer get depressed.

4. Stop Arguing

Proverbs 17:14 *Starting a quarrel is like breaching a dam; so drop the matter before a dispute breaks out.*

I was counseling a couple that had a history of arguing about most anything. One such argument occurred while visiting friends in a town about two hundred miles away. The husband became so angry that he left the friends house and drove back home, yes, two hundred miles away. He did not tell his wife what he was going to do when he stormed out!

His wife thought he was cooling off so she waited before calling him. He answered the phone but he was already 100 miles away. He told her to find her own way back!

Two days later they came in for an emergency session. I asked the husband to explain what the argument was about. He took forty-five minutes to explain the disagreement in great detail.

When it was my turn to speak, I told him he did a masterful job laying out why they had argued. I said but their was one problem with your explanation, "You both argued about your disagreement!"

A major theme of failing relationships is arguing. What the argument centers on varies from minor to major.

It doesn't matter what the disagreement is over, what matters is that the issue becomes a problem. Instead of discussing a matter objectively two people engage in making, proving, or defending their point.

The goal becomes winning your point instead of coming to an agreement ... and the relationship is damaged. Don't think that the damage is for a moment, but in fact the damage can last for years.

Routine arguing leaves a residue of resentment that builds up over time and will eventually reduce the feelings you have for the other person or destroy the relationship completely.

Scripture Forbids Arguing

Proverbs 15:18 *A hot-tempered man stirs up dissension, but a patient man calms a quarrel.*

Proverbs 17:19 *He who loves a quarrel loves sin; he who builds a high gate invites destruction.*

Proverbs 16:32 *Better to be patient than powerful; better to have self-control than to conquer a city.*

Ephesians 4:29 *Let no corrupt communication proceed out of your mouth, but that which is good to the use of edifying, that it may minister grace unto the hearers.*

My Plan To
Keep The Peace

God places a high value on keeping the peace. When you participate in an argument you are contributing to disturbing the peace.

Romans 12:18 *If it is possible, as far as it depends on you, live at peace with everyone.*

II Thessalonians 3:16 *Now may the Lord of peace himself give you peace at all times in every way. The Lord be with you all.*

Matthew 5:9 *Blessed are the peacemakers, for they shall be called sons of God.*

John 14:27 *Peace I leave with you; my peace I give to you. Not as the world gives do I give to you. Let not your hearts be troubled, neither let them be afraid.*

Hebrews 12:14 *Strive for peace with everyone, and for the holiness without which no one will see the Lord.*

I Corinthians 14:33 *For God is not a God of confusion but of peace. As in all the churches of the saints,*

I Peter 3:9-11 *Do not repay evil for evil or reviling for reviling, but on the contrary, bless, for to this you were called, that you may obtain a blessing. For "Whoever desires to love life and see good days, let him keep his tongue from evil and his lips from speaking deceit; let him turn away from evil and do good; let him seek peace and pursue it.*

The message is clear, do not argue, keep the peace.

149

My Plan To
Stop Arguing

1. **Goal**: My goal is to not argue.

2. **Reminder**. We need to be told once but reminded often. Write this verse on a 3x5 card and keep it with you:

> **Proverbs 17:14** *Starting a quarrel is like breaching a dam; so drop the matter before a dispute breaks out. the sun go down on your wrath.*

3. Action. When you realize that you want to argue—**STOP** and **REPLACE** your thoughts by reciting the verse.

When you **STOP** and **REPLACE** your negative thoughts with the verse you are establishing a new way of thinking (making a new habit) and you are one step closer to being transformed as stated in Romans 12:2. Keep working on it and do not be discouraged. It takes time. Ask God to help you.

> **Romans 8:26** *Likewise the Spirit also helps in our weaknesses. For we do not know what we should pray for as we ought, but the Spirit Himself makes intercession for us with groanings which cannot be uttered.*

Do your best to not argue. You will know you are transformed when you no longer want to argue.

5. Stop Using Harmful Language

Ephesians 4:29 *Let no corrupt word proceed out of your mouth, but what is good for necessary edification, that it may impart grace to the hearers.*

Corrupt The greek word translated *corrupt* means; *rotten, no longer fit for use, worthless* (*Thayer's Greek Definitions*).

Paul is telling believers to stop using speech that is destructive, impure, dishonest, or degrading—anything that tears others down.

Words can convey empathy, understanding, and trust, or conversely, sarcasm, impatience, or disrespect.

Tone of Voice Listeners interpret intent and emotion through your tone of voice more than actual words. The same sentence can be perceived as supportive or critical depending on how it is spoken.

Edification Christians should use words to build up people rather than to tear them down. Your words should give grace (help) in the sense that they build people up and communicate encouragement. Your words should be pleasant to the hearer.

The Bible has a lot to say about speech, words, and how we use them—emphasizing that our words have great power for both good and harm. Here are some key verses:

Matthew 15:11 *Not what goes into the mouth defiles a man; but what comes out of the mouth, this defiles a man.*

Here, Jesus is responding to criticism from the Pharisees and scribes who were upset that His disciples did not follow the traditional Jewish ritual of handwashing before eating (see Matthew 15:1–2). Those rituals were part of the oral tradition not Scripture. Later, in Matthew 15:18–19, Jesus explains further:

But what comes out of the mouth proceeds from the heart, and this defiles a person. For out of the heart come evil thoughts, murder, adultery, sexual immorality, theft, false witness, slander.

God is more concerned with your heart than with external appearances. What you say and how you treat others reflect your inner spiritual condition.

Guard your speech and thoughts, because they reveal your heart's alignment with God. Your speech can build up or destroy; it carries real consequences.

Proverbs 18:21 *Death and life are in the power of the tongue, and those who love it will eat its fruit.*

Proverbs 21:23 *Those who guard their mouths and their tongues keep themselves from calamity.*

Proverbs 16:28 *A perverse person stirs up conflict, and a gossip separates close friends.*

Ephesians 4:25 *Therefore each of you must put off falsehood and speak truthfully to your neighbor.*

Colossians 4:6 *Let your conversation be always full of grace, seasoned with salt, so that you may know how to answer everyone.*

James 3:5–6 *The tongue is a small part of the body, but it makes great boasts. Consider what a great forest is set on fire by a small spark.*

To change your communication habits become aware and do the following:

1. **Pause** before speaking. Ask yourself:

> Is it true?
> Is it kind?
> Is it necessary?

2. **Replace**, don't just remove negative words, use encouraging words. Instead of sarcasm, use honesty with compassion.

3. **Remember**, the tone of your voice should be kind and pleasant.

4. **Apologize and correct**. When harmful words slip out, take responsibility and make amends—it rebuilds trust and humility.

5. **Practice gratitude.** Grateful people naturally speak more kindly and optimistically.

My Plan To Always Speak Kindly To Others

1. **Goal**: My goal is to speak words that are kind and encouraging.

2. **Reminder**. We need to be told once but reminded often. Write this verse on a 3x5 card and keep it with you:

> **Ephesians 4:29** *Let no corrupt word proceed out of your mouth, but what is good for necessary edification, that it may impart grace to the hearers.*

3. **Action**. When you realize that you are thinking of saying something harmful—**STOP** and **REPLACE** your thoughts by reciting the verse. Say something encouraging.

When you **STOP** and **REPLACE** your negative thoughts with the verse you are establishing a new way of thinking (making a new habit) and you are one step closer to being transformed as stated in Romans 12:2. Keep working on it and do not be discouraged. It takes time. Ask God to help you.

> **Romans 8:26** *Likewise the Spirit also helps in our weaknesses. For we do not know what we should pray for as we ought, but the Spirit Himself makes intercession for us with groanings which cannot be uttered.*

Spoken words are not just important, they reflect the heart of the person using them. Do your best to not speak words that could be harmful. Be sure that your tone of voce is pleasant. You will know you are transformed when you always say things that are uplifting to others.

Chapter 20

What To *Start* Doing

To gain *control* over what you think feel and do you need to *renovate* the way you think.

There are things you need to *start* doing. This will take time, lots of time. It's not going to be easy or quick. If you begin doing what God has said you will slowly change into a different person who is in control of "self."

1. Love Unconditionally

I Corinthians 13:4-8 *Love suffers long and is kind; love does not envy; love does not parade itself, is not puffed up; 5 does not behave rudely, does not seek its own, is not provoked, thinks no evil; 6 does not rejoice in iniquity, but rejoices in the truth; 7 bears all things, believes all things, hopes all things, endures all things.*

Loving others unconditionally is best for you. Without unconditional love, relationships can stay shallow or transactional. Vulnerability and authenticity become risky, limiting emotional intimacy. Judging others constantly by conditions can lead to chronic dissatisfaction and a lack of peace because few people will ever meet your every expectation.

Over time, love with conditions will push people away, especially when they realize love has a price. This will leave you isolated.

When love is conditional, it often aligns with favoritism— "I only love those like me."

A society without unconditional love becomes punitive and unforgiving, which stifles growth, healing, and second chances.

While loving unconditionally is the goal, it's not always appropriate to apply in every situation. Boundaries are essential, especially in relationships with harmful or abusive individuals.

John 13:34 You are to love others because He loves you:

A new command I give you: Love one another.
As I have loved you, so you must love one another.

How Love Behaves

1. Love is **patient** - Love never takes the opportunity to avenge itself.
2. Love is **kind** - Love never offends, insults or says anything unkind.
3. Love is **not jealous** - Love does not desire what another person has in an evil way.
4. Love **does not brag** - Love does not draw attention to itself.
5. Love is **not puffed up** - Love does not have a superior attitude.
6. Love is **not rude** - Love has good manners and makes you feel comfortable.
7. Love **seeks not its own** - Love does not trade being right for another person's feelings.
8. Love is **not provoked** - Love does not get irritated.
9. Love **thinks no evil** - Love does not keep an account of evil deeds, it forgives.
10. Love **does not rejoice over another's fault** - Love rejoices in the truth.
11. Love **covers sin** - Love is able to overlook any sin.
12. Love **always believes the best** - Love looks at facts, not rumors.
13. Love **always looks on the bright side** - Love is never pessimistic.
14. Love **sustains you through suffering** - Love remains steadfast in the face of unpleasant circumstances.
15. Love **will never run in defeat** - Love never gives up.

I Corinthians 13:4-8 Summary
by Dr. Tom Constable

Love does not deal with other people in a way that injures their dignity. It does not insist on having its own way, nor does it put it's own interest before the needs of others. Love is not irritable or touchy, and it *absorbs* offenses, insults, and inconveniences for the sake of others' welfare. It does not keep a record of offenses received to pay them back.

My Plan To Love People Unconditionally

1. Goal: My goal is to love people unconditionally.

2. Reminder. We need to be told once but reminded often. Write this verse on a 3x5 card and keep it with you:

> **I Corinthians 13:4-8** *Love suffers long and is kind; love does not envy; love does not parade itself, is not puffed up; 5 does not behave rudely, does not seek its own, is not provoked, thinks no evil; 6 does not rejoice in iniquity, but rejoices in the truth; 7 bears all things, believes all things, hopes all things, endures all things.*

The following four descriptions of love represent what people struggle with most often. Write these on a 3x5 card and practice them every chance you get. Love is...

Kind - Love never offends, insults or says anything unkind.

Not provoked - Love does not get irritated.

Not rude - Love has good manners and makes you feel comfortable.

Seeks not its own - Love does not trade being right for another person's feelings.

3. Action. When tempted to be unloving—**STOP** and **REPLACE** your thoughts by reciting the verse or one of the four descriptions listed above and choose to show love.

It will take time. When you **STOP** and **REPLACE** your negative thoughts you are establishing a new way of thinking (making a new habit) and you are one step closer to being transformed as stated in Romans 12:2. Keep working on it. Do not be discouraged. Ask God to help you.

> **Romans 8:26** *Likewise the Spirit also helps in our weaknesses. For we do not know what we should pray for as we ought, but the Spirit Himself makes intercession for us with groanings which cannot be uttered.*

You will know you are transformed when you show unconditional love to others consistently.

2. Forgive Others

Ephesians 4:32 *Be kind and compassionate to one another, forgiving each other, just as in Christ, God forgave you.*

A lack of forgiving someone can be the foundation of mental and emotional issues.

A lack of forgiveness can have significant emotional, psychological, and even physical consequences on the person withholding forgiveness. Here's what it can lead to:

Resentment and bitterness. Holding on to anger or resentment can become a heavy emotional weight, often more painful for the person carrying it than for the one who caused the harm. The ongoing stress of replaying a hurtful event or nursing a grudge can keep you in a heightened state of emotional tension.

Mental health effects. Unforgiveness can feed into cycles of constantly thinking about the wrong which is linked to anxiety and depression. Holding on to unforgiveness may shape a person's view of themselves and others, increasing feelings of victimization or helplessness.

Physical health effects. Chronic stress from holding a grudge activates the body's stress response, which can lead to higher blood pressure, and cardiovascular strain. Emotional stress impairs the immune system, making the body more vulnerable to illness.

Relationship damage. A lack of forgiveness can lead to withdrawal from relationships, limiting emotional intimacy.

Isolation. The refusal to let go of past hurts will cause a person to cut off connections or push others away to avoid vulnerability.

Stalled personal growth. Without forgiveness, emotional wounds often stay open, preventing healing.

Inhibited empathy and compassion. Harboring anger will narrow a person's perspective and make it harder to understand or care about others' experiences or feelings.

Withholding forgiveness tends to harm the person doing the withholding more than anyone else. It can trap you in a cycle of pain, prevent emotional healing, and affect your overall well-being. Forgiveness doesn't mean forgetting or condoning wrongdoing—it means forgive and let God deal with the wrongdoer.

Remember, God loved you so much that He forgave you of all your sin when you became a believer. Therefore ...

Ephesians 4:32 *Be kind and compassionate to one another, forgiving each other, just as in Christ, God forgave you.*

What can anyone do to you that is greater than what you and I did to Christ? Because of your sin, and my sin, He went to the cross. What right do you have, or me, to not forgive someone when Jesus has forgiven us of much greater sin? There are no conditions or limits to forgiveness.

> **Matthew 18:21-22** *Then Peter came up and said to Him, "Lord, how often will my brother sin against me, and I forgive him? As many as seven times?" Jesus said to him, "I do not say to you seven times, but seventy times seven.*

Reminder: Matthew 6:15, Jesus states,

> *But if you do not forgive others their sins, your Father will not forgive your sins.*

Jesus is saying that forgiveness has no conditions or limits. Continue to forgive, again, and again, and again, keep on forgiving. That's the way God treats you.

My Plan To
Forgive Others

1. Goal: My goal is to forgive others for wrongdoing toward me.

2. Reminder. We need to be told once but reminded often. Write this verse on a 3x5 card and keep it with you:

Ephesians 4:32. *Be kind and compassionate to one another, forgiving each other, just as in Christ, God forgave you.*

3. Action. When you are tempted to not forgive—**STOP** and **REPLACE** your thoughts by reciting the verse.

When you **STOP** and **REPLACE** your negative thoughts with the verse you are establishing a new way of thinking (making a new habit) and you are one step closer to being transformed as stated in Romans 12:2. Keep working on it and do not be discouraged. It takes time. Ask God to help you.

Romans 8:26 *Likewise the Spirit also helps in our weaknesses. For we do not know what we should pray for as we ought, but the Spirit Himself makes intercession for us with groanings which cannot be uttered.*

You will know that you are transformed when you establish the habit of forgiving others of their wrongdoing.

3. Show Grace To Others

Ephesians 2:8-9 *For by grace you have been saved through faith, and that not of yourselves; it is the gift of God, not of works, lest anyone should boast.*

Grace means **unmerited favor**. Grace is not earned through good deeds or human effort. It is a gift freely given by God to you.

Since God showered you with His grace when you became a Christian, you are to show grace to others out of gratitude. As a believer you are called to forgive as you have been forgiven—not based on whether the other person deserves it, but because grace was first shown to you.

Ephesians 4:32 *Be kind and compassionate to one another, forgiving each other, just as in Christ God forgave you.*

Examples of Grace in The Bible

The prodigal son (Luke 15:11–32)
A son demands his inheritance early, squanders it, and hits rock bottom. When he returns home expecting judgment, his father runs to him, embraces him, and throws a party. The father doesn't punish or lecture—he forgives and restores his son with love.

Jesus and the woman caught in adultery (John 8:1–11)
Religious leaders bring a woman caught in adultery to Jesus, expecting him to condemn her. Instead, Jesus says,

165

Let the one without sin cast the first stone. When no one does, he tells her, *Neither do I condemn you. Go and sin no more.* Jesus forgives her and invites her to a changed life—not because she deserves it, but out of mercy and grace.

Peter denied the lord three times (Mark 14:66 -16:20)
Mark's record of the account tells how Peter denied the Lord three times the night before He was crucified. When the three women arrived at the tomb three days later to anoint Jesus with spices they discovered that He was gone. An angel told them that He is risen! Then, the angel told them to go tell the disciples ... and Peter!

What a demonstration of God's Grace! Peter had denied the Lord three times before He was crucified and God The Father told the angel to tell Mary to be sure to tell ... **Peter!**

God showed Grace to Peter after His darkest moment. God shows that same Grace to you. Show that same Grace to others.

My Plan To Show Grace To Others Every Chance I Get

1. Goal: My goal is to show grace to others every chance I get..

2. Reminder. We need to be told once but reminded often. Write this verse on a 3x5 card and keep it with you:

> **Galatians 6:10** *Therefore, as we have opportunity, let us do good to all, especially to those who are of the household of faith.*

3. Action. When you are tempted to withhold showing grace to someone—**STOP** and **REPLACE** your thoughts by reciting the verse.

When you **STOP** and **REPLACE** your negative thoughts with the verse you are establishing a new way of thinking (making a new habit) and you are one step closer to being transformed as stated in Romans 12:2. Keep working on it and do not be discouraged. It takes time. Ask God to help you.

> **Romans 8:26** *Likewise the Spirit also helps in our weaknesses. For we do not know what we should pray for as we ought, but the Spirit Himself makes intercession for us with groanings which cannot be uttered.*

You will know you are transformed when you show grace to others every chance you get.

4. Have Boundaries

Proverbs 4:23-27 *Keep your heart with all diligence, For out of it spring the issues of life. 24 Put away from you a deceitful mouth, And put perverse lips far from you. 25 Let your eyes look straight ahead, And your eyelids look right before you. 26 Ponder the path of your feet, And let all your ways be established. 27 Do not turn to the right or the left; Remove your foot from evil.*

Boundaries are critical! We have seen what can happen when a river overflows it's banks or boundaries. I'm writing this in 2025 and just last year in North Carolina Hurricane Helene poured up to 31 inches of rain in the state causing catastrophic damage and tremendous loss of life. And just this year so much rain fell in the hill country of south Texas that the Guadalupe River rose 26 feet in 45 minutes. Another catastrophic event that caused enormous damage and at least 135 people lost their lives.

Boundaries prevent extreme behavior. An obvious contributor to failing to have self-control is a lack of having clearly defined boundaries. If you have not decided what you will *not do* you are opening yourself up to doing most anything!

King Solomon gave his son instructions (Proverbs 1:8) on how to live a successful life when he wrote the book of Proverbs around 3,000 years ago!

In Proverbs 4:23 the Hebrew word for "Keep" means "to guard from dangers" according to the *Brown, Driver, and Briggs Hebrew Lexicon.* "Keep" is also a command, so Solomon is commanding his son to guard his "heart" from dangers. The Hebrew word for "heart" represents mind, emotion, and will.

Why is guarding what you think so important? Because what you think determines what you will do or not do. Solomon says that *For out of it* [your heart] *spring the issues of life.* The word for *issues* means boundaries or borders. The word is used to mark off a territory or city.

Solomon will now tell us exactly what boundaries you need to guard in 4:24-27:

1. v24 Guard what you **say.**
Put away from you a deceitful mouth, And put perverse lips far from you.

The Apostle Paul said it this way in **Ephesians 4:29** *Let no corrupt word proceed out of your mouth, but what is good for necessary edification, that it may impart grace to the hearers.*

2. v25 Guard what you **see.**
Let your eyes look straight ahead, And your eyelids look right before you.
3. v26 Guard where you **go.**
Ponder the path of your feet, And let all your ways be established.
4. v27 Guard yourself from **evil.** *Do not turn to the right or the left; Remove your foot from evil.*

What you can do:

> Be aware of what you allow into your mind through the media, conversations, environments.
>
> Filter influences through your values and beliefs.
>
> Cultivate inner integrity, compassion, and self-awareness through prayer, reflection, or journaling.

Watch your words (v. 24) Words have power to hurt or heal.

> Speak truthfully and kindly.
> Avoid gossip, crude humor, or dishonest speech.
> Stay silence when tempted to say something harmful.

Stay focused (v. 25)

> Distractions and temptations can pull you off course.

Set clear life goals or spiritual priorities.

Stay focused on your purpose—avoid comparing yourself to others.

I Have Boundaries

1. Goal: My goal is to guard my heart with boundaries.

2. Reminder. We need to be told once but reminded often. Write this verse on a 3x5 card and keep it with you:

> **Proverbs 4:23** *Keep your heart with all diligence, For out of it spring the issues of life.*

3. Action. When you are tempted to violate your boundaries — **STOP** and **REPLACE** your thoughts by reciting the verse.

When you **STOP** and **REPLACE** your negative thoughts with the verse you are establishing a new way of thinking (making a new habit) and you are one step closer to being transformed as stated in Romans 12:2. Keep working on it and do not be discouraged. It takes time. Ask God to help you.

> **Romans 8:26** *Likewise the Spirit also helps in our weaknesses. For we do not know what we should pray for as we ought, but the Spirit Himself makes intercession for us with groanings which cannot be uttered.*

You will know you are transformed when you do not violate your boundaries.

171

5. Stand Firm

Philippians 4:8-9 *Finally, brethren, whatever things are true, whatever things are noble, whatever things are just, whatever things are pure, whatever things are lovely, whatever things are of good report, if there is any virtue and if there is anything praiseworthy—meditate on these things. 9 The things which you learned and received and heard and saw in me, these do, and the God of peace will be with you.*

The Apostle Paul told the believers in the city of Philippi twice to "stand firm" (Philippians 1:27 and 4:1). Apparently they had issues with internal struggles, conflicts, and anxieties. In order to "stand firm" the believers were to get their thinking straight so they would not give in to the difficulties they were having. Paul listed what they needed to "think" about in order to "stand firm" and not be overwhelmed with life events in 4:8-9.

> *Reminder* I addressed the need to change what you think in Chapter 19, beginning on page 126. What you think about is a core issues of this book. The Bible often addresses the need to control your thoughts because what you dwell on and imagine shapes your actions, character, and spiritual health.
>   If you want to change the direction your life then practice the previous things to stop doing and start doing until they become a part of who people know you to be.

Here's the list of things Paul wants us to think about, and their meaning, in order to "stand firm":

1. *true* refers to what aligns with God's truth, not deception
2. *noble* refers to what is dignified and morally right.
3. *just* (right) refers to what conforms to God's standards.
4. *pure* refers to what is morally clean, unmixed with sin.
5. *lovely* refers to what draws affection toward what is good.
6. *of good report* refers to what has a good reputation.
7. *virtue* refers to moral and spiritual quality.
8. *praisworthy* refers to what God approves, not what flatters self.

The word translated *meditate* means to "practise", that is, to perform repeatedly or habitually everything Paul just listed.

Paul is not saying ignore reality, but discipline your thoughts so they are shaped by what God said to do rather than anxiety, sin, or out of uncontrolled thinking.

> *J.B. Phillips New Testament* says it this way (this is a transliteration and not a word for word translation which means that Phillips tried to capture the meaning of what Paul intended):
>
> > *Here is a last piece of advice. If you believe in goodness and if you value the approval of God, fix your minds on the things which are holy and right and pure and beautiful and good.*

If you were to discipline your thinking as Paul directs, you would never develop a "disorder" and you would be able to reverse the struggles you are now having regardless of what it is.

Paul listed what we need to "think" about in order to "stand firm" and not be overwhelmed with life events.

I Stand Firm

1. Goal: My goal is to stan firm.

2. Reminder. We need to be told once but reminded often. Write this verse on a 3x5 card and keep it with you:

> **Philippans 4:8** *Finally, brethren, whatever things are true, whatever things are noble, whatever things are just, whatever things are pure, whatever things are lovely, whatever things are of good report, if there is any virtue and if there is anything praiseworthy—meditate on these things.*

3. Action. When you are tempted to think wrong thoughts—**STOP** and **REPLACE** your thoughts by reciting the verse.

When you **STOP** and **REPLACE** your negative thoughts with the verse you are establishing a new way of thinking (making a new habit) and you are one step closer to being transformed as stated in Romans 12:2. Keep working on it and do not be discouraged. It takes time. Ask God to help you.

> **Romans 8:26** *Likewise the Spirit also helps in our weaknesses. For we do not know what we should pray for as we ought, but the Spirit Himself makes intercession for us with groanings which cannot be uttered.*

You will know you are transformed when you are able to consistently stand firm.

174

Chapter 25

BIPOLAR

Have you been diagnosis as bipolar? If so, this chapter is for you and it is good news!

Acording to the DSM-V the bipolar disorder is a mental health condition characterized by mood swings that include emotional highs (mania) and lows (depression).

According to the Mayo Clinic website the cause of bipolar is unknown. They state that the condition is likely caused by a combination of genetics and faulty brain chemistry (see page 25). Medications are suggested to treat symptoms.

Since the issues of genetics and brain chemistry has never been proven, as discussed earlier, there is another explanation.

The symptoms of bipolar can be explained by understanding the natural and normal tendencies of the Sanguine-Melancholy temperament.

Natural tendencies Temperament represents the natural tendencies with which you were born. The Sanguine-Melancholy is a combination of Sanguine (extroverted, people person), and Melancholy (introverted, private person. The natural tendency of this blend is to want to be with people *most* of the time and by themselves *some* of the time.

You can suddenly go from being with others and engaged to the need to be alone. This is a natural "mood shift" to satisfy the need to be alone. If you have not had enough alone time you can become irritated, rude, and snap at those close by, and/ or withdraw.

Emotional range As a Sanguine-Melancholy you have the highest emotional range of all temperament combinations. This emotional presence means you are capable of expressing the greatest excitement and feel the deepest despair. Without controlling your emotions you naturally exhibit mood swings that can be anywhere from mild to severe.

Sensitive Your emotional capability causes you to be very sensitive to what others say or think about you. You may react to perceived criticism with a strong verbal defense.

Creative The Sanguine-Melancholy is by far the most creative of all the temperament blends. Your creativity can be in art, music, problem solving, etc. You tend to have great writing ability that shows up in stories, poetry, and writing songs.

High drive to win You are driven to do a task correctly and make a good impression in the process. You are capable of being the top in your chosen field.

Cause The cause of the bipolar diagnosis is a natural capability with which you are born that is not being controlled.

Being labeled bipolar has nothing to do with a bipolar gene or brain chemistry being low on neurotramitters. It is an issue of a lack of self-control of natural tendencies. This is good news because the symptoms of bipolar are within your ability to control without medication. If you are currently using medication you must follow the directions of your provider to modify it's use.

How to Control The
Sanguine-Melancholy Tendencies

1. Your need to be with, near, or around other people is *normal*, natural, and necessary. But it's limited. Once your natural need to be around people is met for the day, you need to be alone. You have noticed that when you have been with others you suddenly feel the need to leave. Accept this is normal.

2. The need to be alone is also *normal*, natural, and necessary. You cannot function efficiently without sufficient alone time everyday. This too is okay.

3. The third important thing to manage is having a plan. You function best when you have a plan, usually a detailed plan. For example, you need to know where you are going, what you need to do when there, who is going to be there, when will you leave, etc. Once there, you will need warm up time if new people are present.

4. The greatest task is to overcome the fear of rejection and the need to look favorable in the eyes of others.

To prevent emotional reactions to life events or people's negative comments understand and apply Romans 8:28-29.

As a Christian, accept that every event in your life is used by God to help conform you into the image of Christ. Even being rejected and/or made to look unfavorable in the eyes of others can be used by God to help you grow spiritually.

Romans 8:28 *And we know that in all things God works for the good of those who love him, who have been called according to his purpose.*

So, God does not do anything **to** you but **for** you. If you would view life through this verse, and do the things covered in the previous chapters, mood swings would not occur.

When you think you may be, or have been rejected, or made to look unfavorable in the eyes of others, trust that God is working in your life. Do not react. By getting upset and emotional you are doing what the saints were doing when the Apostle John wrote John 12:42-43:

Nevertheless even among the rulers many believed in Him, but because of the Pharisees they did not confess Him, lest they should be put out of the synagogue; 43 for they loved the praise of men more than the praise of God.

Here, the behavior of new believers was determined by what others might do to them. They did not admit their new faith in Christ because they were afriad they would be kicked out of the synagogue. They were more concerned to have the approval of men than to have the approval of God.

The lesson? Don't be concerned about what others will say or do, please God

My Plan To Stop
Having Mood Swings

1. Goal: My goal is to stop having mood swings.

2. Reminder. We need to be told once but reminded often. Write this verse on a 3x5 card and keep it with you:

> **Romans 8:28** *And we know that in all things God works for the good of those who love him, who have been called according to his purpose.*

3. Action. When you are starting to feel rejected—**STOP** and **REPLACE** your thoughts by reciting the verse.

When you **STOP** and **REPLACE** your negative thoughts with the verse you are establishing a new way of thinking (making a new habit) and you are one step closer to being transformed as stated in Romans 12:2. Keep working on it and do not be discouraged. It takes time. Ask God to help you.

> **Romans 8:26** *Likewise the Spirit also helps in our weaknesses. For we do not know what we should pray for as we ought, but the Spirit Himself makes intercession for us with groanings which cannot be uttered.*

Do your best to not react to the possibility of being rejected. You will know you are transformed when you no longer react to the feeling of being rejected.

Chapter 22

How Do I Know If I'm Making Progress?

There are four ways to know if you are making progress on your new journey.

Awareness Becoming aware of what you need to correct cannot be overstated. We move through life doing things that we are not aware of until something happens to awaken us. Many have said to me "I didn't realize I was doing that!"

Acceptance Once aware it is necessary to accept that you need to change. "Yes, I do that!"

Change The third and most difficult part is to decide to change. You can be aware and accept that you are doing something that you need to fix and never change. "I've decided to change."

Reaction Time Growth is directly related to how long it takes you to respond Biblically to a negative event.

How Long Does It Take You To Adjust?

Disturbing Event   Biblical Response

↓   **Time**   ↓
▬▬▬▬▬▬▬▬▬▬▬ **?** ▬▬▬▬▬▬▬▬▬▬▬

Your reaction time is how long it takes you to **stop** the negative thinking, feeling, doing, and saying, and **replace** it with what God said to do.

For example, if you were to say something harmful to someone and you normally wait a week to ask for forgiveness but you're working on it so, instead of 7 days you do it in 6. That's progress! Keep working on it and you will reduce your reaction time form 6 to 5 to 4 to 3 to 2 to 1 to hours, minutes, and seconds. You will eventually not react at all because you are transformed.

Chapter 24

Conclusion

What causes the issues discussed in this book and what is the best way to deal with them?

If you follow man's wisdom, specifically the medical model, you end up believing that your issue is not your fault. You are a victim of your environment, faulty brain chemistry or you inherited some bad genes. Your struggle is considered a disease and is treated as such. This is frankly a lie since the medical model has never been proven, it remains just a theory. The medical model is the most widely used to treat so-called mental disorders. Man's wisdom misleads people who are struggling with mental, emotional, or behavioral issues.

God's wisdom offers simple and practical answers as to why people struggle. The Bible says, metaphorically, if you want to know the cause of your issues look in the mirror.

God says we are responsible for what we think, feel, do, and say. My choices are the cause of my struggle.

You have the freedom to choose to be anxious, angry, and argue, you can choose to get depressed, and use harmful language. It's a choice to love others, forgive, show grace, have boundaries on what you will and will not do. It's your choice to stand firm.

If you make different choices you can reverse any issue with which you are struggling. Romans 8:5-6 puts it his way.

5 For those who live according to the flesh set their minds on the things of the flesh, but those who live according to the Spirit, the things of the Spirit. 6 For to be carnally minded is death, but to be spiritually minded is life and peace. 7 Because the carnal mind is enmity against God; for it is not subject to the law of God, nor indeed can be. 8 So then, those who are in the flesh cannot please God.

In this passage, the Apostle Paul contrasts two ways of living: "according to the flesh" and "according to the Spirit." The greek word translated "death" does not mean physical death but spiritual separation from God. If you live your life according to the way you believe and not God's way, then you will not have fellowship with God.

Behind every issue is the choice to respond to people and life events your way. It's what seems right to you which is living according to the flesh. Living according to the Spirit (God's way) you will not and cannot develop an issue as discussed in this book. You can also reverse any issue you may be having.

What is your mind set on?

About The Author

John T. Cocoris has devoted his life since the 1970s to develop the temperament model of behavior. John has a B.A. from Tennessee Temple University, a Masters of Theology (Th. M.) from Dallas Theological Seminary, a Masters in Counseling (M.A.) from Amberton University, and a Doctorate in Psychology (Psy.D.) from California Coast University. John was a licensed therapist in the state of Texas from 1995-2020.

John established Profile Dynamics in the early 1980s to develop and promote the temperament model of behavior for use in business and counseling. He has been a management consultant since 1984 and has worked with a variety of companies giving seminars for training managers and sales people.

John has conducted seminars in churches to help church counselors help others. John has also trained other therapists in the use of the temperament model in counseling. John has been interviewed on the radio and has been featured numerous times on COPE, a national cable TV talk show.

John and Phillip Moss formed Temperament Dynamics, LLC in 2017 to further develop, expand, and promote the temperament model of behavior.

John has written many books and manuals about the temperament model including: *Why We Do What We Do, New Insights Into The Temperament Model of Behavior; Born With A Creative Temperament, The Sanguine-Melancholy; 7 Steps To A Better You, How To Develop Your Natural Tendencies; A Parent's Manual To Helping Your Child Develop Their Natural Temperament Tendencies; A Therapist's Guide to The Temperament Model of Behavior; A Leader's Guide To Using The Temperament Model of Behavior; How To Sell Using The Temperament Model of Behavior; The DISCII, DISC3, DISC Strengths, and Four Temperaments Assessments, and The Temperament Profile Assessment User's Guide.*